About the Book

Here is the thrilling story of one of the most important battles of World War II. With richness of historical detail author Charles Mercer recreates the great naval battle in which vastly outnumbered American naval forces sought out the Japanese Imperial Fleet. The outcome of the war in the Pacific hung in the balance. Mercer, who served as an intelligence officer in the Pacific during World War II, presents absorbingly the background that began with the treacherous Japanese attack on Pearl Harbor. Lucidly and simply *Miracle at Midway* explains the causes of a war the United States hoped to avoid but fought valiantly after being attacked.

MIRACLE
AT
MIDWAY

by Charles Mercer

G. P. PUTNAM'S SONS, NEW YORK

Library of Congress Cataloging in Publication Data
Mercer, Charles E.
Miracle at Midway.
Includes bibliographical references and index.
SUMMARY: Recreates the naval battle between Japanese
and American forces which was the decisive factor in the
Pacific theater during World War II.
1. Midway, Battle of, 1942—Juvenile literature.
[1. Midway, Battle of, 1942. 2. World War, 1939-1945—
Naval operations, American] I. Title.
D774.M5M47   940.54'26   77-24116
ISBN 0-399-20612-4

Contents

Everything is very simple in War, but the simplest thing is difficult. These difficulties accumulate and produce a friction which no man can imagine exactly who has not seen War.

—General Karl von Clausewitz, *On War*

1

Puzzling Events

Usually the great American naval base at Pearl Harbor in Hawaii was a busy, noisy place. On Sunday mornings, however, when most people slept late, it became as quiet as a country cemetery.

The morning of December 7, 1941, seemed no different from any other early Sunday. Light grew quickly over the blue reaches of the big harbor, revealing seventy combat ships and twenty-four other vessels which serviced them. It was a beautiful dawning on the green sugarcane fields of the island of Oahu and its southern harbor, where the United States Pacific Fleet was based. From the city of Honolulu nearby rose the stroke of churchbells calling the faithful. Aboard battleships, cruisers, destroyers and other naval vessels moored in the harbor voices sounded hushed as a red sun rose over the Tantalus Mountains.

It was also quiet at the big American air bases of Oahu—Wheeler Field, Hickam Field, Kaneohe and others. On Sunday mornings bugles did not blare reveille at 5:30 A.M. for soldiers, airmen and marines. Though most were asleep, all anticipated a quick summons to duty at any time. For the American armed forces in Hawaii had been alerted, most recently on November 27, to the threat of war with Japan. At the airfields the chief threat was thought to be from sabotage by local people of Japanese descent who might try to destroy bombers and fighter planes. So the airplanes had been parked wingtip to wingtip out on the strips under the close watch of armed guards.

Serene though all appeared in that dawning of December 7 in Hawaii, some puzzling things were happening.

About forty miles north of Pearl Harbor on Oahu, at Point Opana, two young Army privates were on training duty with one of the half-dozen mobile search radar stations which had recently been brought to the island. This type of air spotting had saved Britain in 1940 when the German air force had tried to gain control of the skies. By means of this device approaching enemy planes appeared as blips on a screen and thus could be located well in advance by defending fliers and anti-aircraft batteries. But it was a new system in Hawaii, and the Army was using it strictly for training. It happened that on Sundays, for no particular reason, the training was carried out between the hours of 4 A.M. and 7 A.M. (0400 to 0700).

That Sunday morning around 0650 the two Army radar men at Opana on the northern point of Oahu plotted the course of a plane coming out of the north where there was nothing but open sea. This information they quickly reported to the radio center at Fort Shafter near Honolulu.

The duty officer there at that hour was a green, sleepy second lieutenant who apparently thought the trainees up at Opana were imagining things and told them to knock off and close their mobile van for the day. But the two privates, fascinated by radar and wanting to improve their skill, remained on duty. And then, at 0702, they saw something so extraordinary on their screen that they cried out in astonishment. Blip after blip—more than one hundred of them —were approaching Oahu from the north!

Excitedly they phoned the information center again. Their excitement infected the switchboard operator, who put their call through to the same sleepy duty officer. But the lieutenant was not impressed by their report of a big flight approaching from the north at about 180 miles per hour.

Forget it, he told them. What they must be seeing was a flight of Army B-17s due to arrive from California that morning. But the lieutenant should have known that flight was composed of only a dozen bombers which would come from the northeast. Once more he told the men to knock off for the day. And young Army recruits, even eager ones, know it's hopeless to try to argue with a second lieutenant. . . .

A few hours earlier, at 0355, the converted minesweeper U.S.S. *Condor,* on routine patrol off Pearl Harbor, had sighted a submarine periscope less than two miles from the harbor entrance. She sent word by blinker to sister destroyer *Ward.* Then the skippers of the two vessels discussed the situation by TBS—Talk Between Ships—radio. Their conversation was overheard by a Navy monitoring station ashore, but nobody there thought it worth passing the report to headquarters. No doubt it was just another erroneous sighting.

But at 0633, as it grew lighter, a Catalina flying boat patrolling off the Pearl Harbor entrance sighted a midget submarine which definitely was not a vessel of the U.S. Navy. The plane dropped smoke pots on the sighting point and alerted *Ward.* The destroyer came charging to the scene, forward guns blazing at the periscope, and depth-bombed and sank the midget at 0645. At 0651 the captain of *Ward* informed naval district headquarters what had happened. But the information did not reach the headquarters duty officer until 0712.

Meanwhile, at 0700, another Catalina bombed and sank another midget submarine a mile off the harbor entrance. All naval officers were under strict orders to transmit all news of action uncoded so as to facilitate spreading the word. But the Catalina's crew must have forgotten that, for they reported the sinking of the second midget in code. By the time the message was decoded and ready for circulation it was 0730.

While it was 0730 at Pearl Harbor, it was 1 P.M. (1300) in Washington. The mood there at that hour among President Franklin D. Roosevelt, Secretary of State Cordell Hull and the military leaders of the nation was one of almost unbearable tension.

For a long time the United States had possessed a great secret weapon in its tense relationship with Japan. The carefully kept American secret was that we had broken the chief Japanese diplomatic and naval codes. (For many years nearly all nations had sent all important messages to embassies and military commands in a great variety of codes.) By being able to read Japanese messages the United States could estimate plans and intentions. To the codebreakers and the very few government leaders who were allowed to read the translated messages it was increasingly evident that Japan was launched on a course leading to war with the United States. But where would Japan start it—and when—and how?

The feeling of the generals and admirals in Washington was that it probably would begin in the Philippines and Southeast Asia. General Douglas MacArthur, commander of American forces in the Far East, had been alerted and replied that his defenses were ready. Alerted, too, were Admiral Husband E. Kimmel, Commander in Chief of the Pacific Fleet at Pearl Harbor, and Army Major General Walter C. Short, responsible for the defense of Hawaii. In November the Japanese sent a special envoy, Saburu Kurusu, to Washington in an effort to settle the differences between their government and the United States. Kurusu appears to have genuinely hoped to avoid war. Japan beseeched the United States to sell it oil. The United States replied it would not unless Japan got out of China. This Japan refused to do. The result was a deadlock between the two nations.

For the very few Americans in the know there was puzzlement in the way the Japanese were changing their naval codes. On November 1 all the encoded call signs of Navy ships, shore facilities and administrative headquarters were abruptly changed. American radio intelligence men began working around the clock to identify 20,000 new call signs. They were making progress when the call signs were changed again on December 1. Another puzzler was that after November 16 Tokyo ceased to exchange messages with all of its aircraft carriers. Japanese diplomatic codes remained unchanged, however.

The immediate cause of the unbearable tension in Washington on that Sunday, December 7, was an encoded diplomatic message which Tokyo had begun sending to its American embassy on December 6. It was a very long message which the special envoys were directed to present to Secretary Hull. Army Intelligence ran the message through its decrypting machines, making it available to the Americans faster than it was to the Japanese. By 1930 on Saturday evening the codebreakers had completed the first thirteen parts of the message— a long list of grievances against the United States—and rushed it to President Roosevelt at the White House with word there was a last part yet to come.

The President finished reading the translation just before midnight, realized that the as yet unreceived last part had to be a command to break diplomatic relations, and said, "This means war!" For reasons not known to this day General George C. Marshall, Army Chief of Staff, and Admiral Harold R. Stark, Chief of Naval Operations, did not receive the report that night from officers supposed to deliver it.

At 0915, Washington time, on Sunday, December 7, the codebreakers brought Admiral Stark the entire message, including the last part which broke off diplomatic relations with the United States. There was no declaration of war, no clue anywhere in the message as to what the Japanese intended to do next. Then, around 1015, the codebreakers rushed to Stark's office an additional paragraph from Tokyo which ordered the envoys to present the message to Secretary Hull at 1300 that day and to *destroy all the embassy's coding machines and secret documents.*

Stark and his staff officers pondered the significance of that 1300 delivery hour to Hull. Gazing at the time chart on a wall, they observed that 1 P.M. in Washington meant 7:30 A.M. in Hawaii. But farther west in Guam and the Philippines, the other American bases which the Japanese might hit, it still would be dark at that hour, thus precluding the possibility of attack in those places.

Stark's intelligence officer urged him to pick up his phone at once, call Admiral Kimmel in Pearl Harbor and warn him of the possibility of a Japanese attack. But Stark refused on grounds another message would be confusing. He said the Army was responsible for the defense of Hawaii, and so Marshall should issue the warning. (The Army–Navy habit of alternately bowing to and jostling each other would plague the war effort to the end.)

General Marshall had not even been informed the long Japanese message existed. But he was told about it as soon as he returned from his customary Sunday morning horseback ride and hastened to Stark's office. There, after quickly studying the situation, he agreed the nation was on the brink of war and Hawaii must be warned. His chief communications officer said General Short could get the word in twenty minutes.

At noon, Washington time—6:30 A.M., Hawaiian time—Marshall sent a message to Short telling him what had happened and warning him:

JUST WHAT SIGNIFICANCE THE HOUR SET MAY HAVE WE DO NOT KNOW, BUT BE ON THE ALERT ACCORDINGLY.

In the next hour General Marshall called the Army communications center three times to make sure the message had been sent. Each time he was assured that indeed it had been. But no one told the General there had been a breakdown in Army radio and the message had gone by commercial Western Union.

At 7:30 A.M., Pearl Harbor time, a Japanese-American Western Union messenger boy, Tadao Fuchikami, was riding his motorbike toward General Short's headquarters with one of the most important messages of the century when all hell broke loose.

2

Calamity

Isoruku Yamamoto, Commander in Chief of the Japanese Combined Fleet, liked Americans and did not want to go to war with them. Americans liked him, too. When he had been attached to the Japanese Embassy in Washington, American officers had respected his naval knowledge, enjoyed his social company and envied his winning ways at poker.

Early in 1941 Minister of War Hideki Tojo assigned Yamamoto the task of deciding the best way to neutralize American naval power in a projected war against the United States. Yamamoto told Prince Fumimaro Konoye, the premier, that it was foolish to contemplate such a war because the industrial and raw material resources of the United States far outstripped Japan's. Konoye did not want war either, but his peace efforts failed. On October 16, 1941, Tojo succeeded Konoye as premier, and from that moment war was inevitable unless the Americans agreed to sell Japan oil.

Meanwhile, Yamamoto worked dutifully on naval attack plans. He knew that Japan must achieve a quick knockout of American seapower and airpower, consolidate its gains and quickly convert the raw materials it seized in the Far East into industrial materials.

His decision on the first move was daring: to destroy the U. S. Pacific Fleet based at Pearl Harbor before war was declared and around the same time smash American air forces in the Philippines and British air forces on the Malay Peninsula.

A Supreme War Council agreed to Yamamoto's plan in September 1941. After the surprise attacks had crippled the Americans and British, the Japanese planned these strategic moves: (1) Conquer swiftly the Philippines, Guam, Wake, Hong Kong, Singapore along with the rest of Malaya and all of the Netherlands East Indies (present-day Indonesia). (2) Develop intensively the entire conquered area's vital resources such as oil, rubber and tin. (3) Create a defensive line protecting this economic empire which would run from the Kurile Islands in the North Pacific through Wake, the Marshall Islands and around the southern and western edges of the Indies and Malaya to the Burma-India border. From bases on this defensive arc the Navy and air forces would isolate Australia and New Zealand from Britain and the United States, which would have to seek peace. (4) Finally, complete the conquest of China, already begun, thus bringing half of the world's people under the control of Japan.

In starting war the Japanese were far stronger in arms, ships, planes and men than everything the Americans could muster against them in the Pacific. What some of their planners other than Yamamoto did not seem to realize, however, was the American capacity to overtake them in time because of far greater industrial capacity—which gives modern war its muscle. They also underestimated the American will to fight to the death if unfairly attacked.

Yamamoto ordered the code changes and screen of silence over the carriers that had perplexed the American codebreakers. He planned carefully the nature of the force which would attack Oahu. It was a powerful one: six of the Imperial Navy's newest and biggest carriers, bearing 423 combat planes; a screening force of nine destroyers and a light cruiser; a support group of two battleships and two heavy cruisers, with three fleet submarines to patrol the flanks and a supply train of eight tankers coming behind. Under cover of darkness the ships of the attack force slipped away from their bases in the homeland and assembled at remote Tankan Bay in the Kuriles.

To lead the Pearl Harbor striking force Yamamoto chose Vice Admiral Chuichi Nagumo, a brave and capable officer who did not like the assignment. Nagumo was under orders to abandon the mission if the force was detected by December 5. Yamamoto believed in the recently developed aircraft carrier—a type of warship which had not yet been tested in combat—as the most effective naval weapon of the time. Thus he directed that the primary targets at Pearl Harbor should be the three American aircraft carriers, all there were in the Pacific Fleet. The other chief targets of the Japanese were the eight American battleships berthed at Pearl.

Nagumo's large task force shaped course from Tankan Bay on November 26 and disappeared into the thick fogs and icy wastes of the North Pacific. One week before that time a huge fleet of 27 submarines sailed from the homeland to station themselves around Oahu. Their task was to sink any ships which escaped from Pearl Harbor into the open sea. Five of these big fleet boats carried midget two-man submarines which had the mission of penerating the harbor and doing all damage possible.

The striking force, rolling down from the north through heavy seas, advanced unobserved. The December 5 deadline for aborting the mission passed, and on December 6 Tokyo sent Nagumo the latest report from the Japanese consulate in Honolulu. To the vast disappointment of the attackers the three American aircraft carriers had left Pearl Harbor, but eight battleships still were there.

The sailors and airmen of the attacking force had been so drugged with propaganda that they were high with the idea of dying for the emperor and killing as many Americans as possible. On the night of December 6 the force went to full speed of 26 knots through a murk of clouds and a heavy swell. While it was still dark the heavy cruisers catapulted two scouting planes to try a reconnaissance of Pearl Harbor. Presumably the radar blip the two Army privates reported from Opana was one of these planes. In any event, the Americans on Oahu were so off guard that the two Japanese scout planes actually flew safely all the way to Pearl and reported back that everything was calm there—not a single ship moving.

It was 0600 and gray light was growing when the force reached the designated launch point about 275 miles north of Pearl. As the attack planes roared off the flight decks of the big carriers, hundreds of crewmen shrieked *"Banzai!"* ("Long life!") in patriotic frenzy. In the first attack wave were 40 torpedo bombers (which the Americans identified as Kates), 49 high-level bombers (Bettys), 51 fighters (Zekes)* and 51 dive-bombers (Vals). It must have been a part of this wave approaching Oahu that the two radar men at Opana sighted and reported to no avail.

When the attackers sighted the coast of Oahu about 0740, they deployed under a careful plan. The fighters were to destroy planes parked on the strips at Wheeler Field. High-level bombers aimed at Hickam Field adjacent to the Pearl Navy Yard. Dive-bombers and torpedo planes headed for Kanehoe and "Battleship Row" where the eight dreadnoughts were moored along the southeast shore of Ford Island, which is located in the chief arm of the harbor. Japanese planning, based on detailed knowledge of the targets, was meticulous. For example, fighters were armed with incendiaries which would set fire to parked planes, while some of the warheads employed by dive-bombers and torpedo planes were heavy enough to pierce battleship armor.

At one moment Pearl Harbor was as peaceful as paradise; at the next it was a flaming hell. A sky that had been a silent well of blue

---

*Codebreakers and many American experts in Japanese arms did not refer to enemy fighters as "Zeros"—a custom of the press—because that identification in messages might be confused with dates or call numbers.

suddenly was filled with planes darting, diving, flying high and low, firing guns and hurling bombs into ships and buildings. At first the Americans were so dazed by the sudden onslaught that no one ever determined to the satisfaction of everyone else precisely when various targets were hit: men being shot at don't have time to look at their watches.

On Ford Island the naval air operations officer had finally got to talking over the phone about those mysterious midget submarines when a bomb came through the roof. He thought it had been dropped by a careless Army bombardier. At Kanehoe on the east coast of the island, where Japanese Vals destroyed 27 of 36 Catalinas, an excited officer phoned Pearl and bleated that the Army had gone berserk and was attacking. At the Wheeler Army base in mid-island, where Zekes blasted rows of parked planes, some thought it was the Navy that had gone berserk. No one was prepared—least of all at many Army antiaircraft emplacements where unmanned guns slanted emptily at a sky suddenly filled with the enemy.

On Battleship Row the crews were in a state of in-port partial readiness. They could not have maintained a higher degree of readiness for any protracted length of time. Thus it should not be inferred that the battleships were hit by the Japanese planes because they did not have enough guns manned and ready.

It happened suddenly. Twelve slow-flying Kates launched torpedoes from altitudes of only 40 to 100 feet at the battleships *Arizona, Tennessee, West Virginia, Maryland* and *Oklahoma*. Four other Kates in a following wave launched more torpedoes at the big ships. At almost the same time Val dive-bombers screamed down, dropping both conventional bombs and others capable of piercing 16-inch armor which smashed through the decks and exploded below. After firing off their lethal bombs and torpedoes, most of the attackers winged around and passed over their targets again, viciously machine gunning sailors on the decks.

Under the smash of torpedoes and crump of heavy bombs exploding below decks the big ships seemed to wince and shudder like humans. Through the cries, the din, the rattle of enemy guns and roar of enemy planes loudspeakers sounded the harsh summons of General Quarters.

Oklahoma was the first battleship victim. She was paired at mooring with *Maryland* and tied outboard of her. A junior grade lieutenant on *Maryland,* awakened by strange sounds, looked out his cabin port. When he had gone to sleep, *Oklahoma* had been there, blocking his view. But now she was gone--and the lieutenant wondered why. Then *Maryland* was shaken by an explosion, and the lieutenant sprang to duty.

Three torpedoes had torn huge holes in *Oklahoma,* which immediately listed 30 degrees. She continued to list before counterflooding measures could be taken to right her. Two more torpedo hits sealed her fate, and she slowly turned turtle while many of her crew clambered aboard *Maryland.* Of 1,354 men aboard *Oklahoma,* 415 died. *Maryland,* taking only two bomb hits, fared better and was the first of the battleships to return to duty.

Arizona, ripped to pieces by bombs and torpedoes, settled so fast after her magazine exploded that hundreds were trapped below. A total of 1,103 of the 1,400 aboard died with their ship. Yet survivors of the racking explosions continued to fire machine guns at enemy planes until the order to abandon rang out. Today a superstructure built over the sunken *Arizona* rises above the waters of Pearl Harbor as a memorial to that December 7 day of disaster.

Quick thinking by the young Officer of the Deck on *West Virginia* saved her from the fate of *Oklahoma.* Upon seeing the first bomb fall, he sounded "Away fire and rescue party!" This alarm brought scrambling to the main deck hundreds of men who would otherwise have been trapped below. *West Virginia* was struck by six torpedoes and two bombs, but swift counterflooding corrected her listing and she settled slowly toward the bottom. Of some 1,500 aboard, 105 were killed.

The captain of *Tennessee,* which was moored inboard of *West*

Virginia, was disemboweled by bomb fragments and died within minutes of the first attack. The crew fought fires all day and, miraculously, only five died.

California, receiving two torpedoes and a bomb hit that exploded her magazine, was saved from capsizing by counterflood measures ordered by a reserve ensign. A total of 98 aboard were killed.

Of the vessels on Battleship Row *Nevada* was the oldest, and her crew conducted themselves with an old-fashioned gallantry that would have warmed Farragut and other naval heroes of the past. When the bombs began to fall, the color guard raised the ensign while the band played "The Star-spangled Banner" and everyone stood at attention. A plane came in, trying to strafe the sailors at attention—and missed them all.

They leaped to battle stations and put up such a hail of fire from machine guns and a five-inch battery that the succeeding waves of Japanese attackers began to exercise care. *Nevada* shot down one and possibly two planes before casting off and heading for the open sea. With a gaping torepdo hole in her side and firing everything she could at a swarm of attackers, she became almost invisible from shore behind a cloud of smoke and spray. Then someone at headquarters ashore, fearing *Nevada* would sink and block the channel, ordered her to drop anchor. This she started to do outside the channel when three more bombs struck her. Old *Nevada,* looking a complete wreck, went aground with 50 men dead. But her appearance was deceiving. Eventually she was towed to the west coast and modernized. She rejoined the Fleet in 1943.

Pennsylvania, flagship of the Fleet, fired all she could at the enemy planes from drydock, took one hit and lost 25 men.

Of the five Japanese midget submarines launched outside Pearl, one actually penetrated into the harbor, whose antisubmarine gate had been left open in one more example of the widespread carelessness. The midget was destroyed by a depth-charge. Two had been sunk outside the harbor, one ran aground and the fifth simply disappeared.

The 27 Japanese fleet submarines stationed around Oahu did no damage.

Soon after the attack began—at 0758, to be precise—Rear Admiral P. N. L. Bellinger, commander of the Fleet's air arm, sent a plain message for all airmen, sailors and soldiers in Hawaii and its area:

AIR RAID, PEARL HARBOR—THIS IS NOT DRILL.

Ships at sea relayed the message, and soon it was being broadcast to stunned civilian listeners in the United States, even as fresh waves of Japanese planes continued to assault Pearl Harbor and the air bases of Oahu.

By 0945, Hawaii time, it was all over. Fires still raged, but at that hour all Japanese attackers were ordered back to their carriers. Only 29 of them had been shot down, though dozens of other planes had been riddled by American marksmen.

When the firing had started, the Japanese-American Western Union messenger boy bearing General Marshall's warning leaped off his bike and sensibly sought cover in a ditch. After things let up a bit he resumed his ride to General Short's headquarters but was stopped by somewhat hysterical military policemen, who decided he was a Japanese saboteur. The young man spent an agonizing time convincing them he was only a patriotic American trying to do his job before they let him pass on with his message.

It was delivered to the headquarters signal office at 1145, and the deciphered message was not delivered to General Short until 1458 —seven hours after the attack. By that time troops had been sent to all the places where they should have been when the attack began. All they succeeded in doing was to shoot down four American planes which were returning to Oahu from the carrier *Enterprise*.

The American losses were tremendous. Nearly 2,400 servicemen had been killed and nearly 1,200 wounded. About 260 planes were destroyed and more than 100 damaged. Seven battleships were sunk or severely damaged, three destroyers wiped out and numerous other vessels left inoperable.

This was war as Americans never had imagined it, coming stealthily, savagely, bent on overwhelming victory through total destruction. Most Americans felt the world never would be the same again. If there had been a bit of chivalry left in existence, it finally had vanished there at Pearl Harbor.

Toward nightfall the pall began to lift, though there remained a stench of oil smoke, cordite, something like putrid meat. Gulls perching on bits of wreckage with oil-smeared wings spread to the dying sun reminded one of vultures. Yet somewhere out there it was a lovely evening. The mountains still were blue, the canefields still swept up the slopes above Aiea in verdant waves while to the south great trade clouds rolled along magnificently detached from the evil affairs of humankind.

3

Aftermath—and Causes

The memorable thing about Pearl Harbor is not the damage done or even the numerous lives lost. Rather, what the Japanese mainly accomplished in their attack was to unite a divided America in implacable fury at their treachery.

Even these many years later it's difficult to find any American who was of high school age or older on December 7, 1941, who cannot tell you precisely what he was doing when news came of the Japanese attack. The event is engraved on the American consciousness because every American's life was immediately, incredibly changed.

American youth of the Vietnam War years in general loathed war and military training no more than did most youths of the 1930s. Disillusionment with the results of World War I had put a mood of isolation on America that left its armed forces ill-prepared for combat. There was a widespread feeling that the British Navy and French Army would take care of any unpleasantness in Europe, and as for the Japanese taking over the Far East—well, their world and welcome to it! So, after Germany started war in Europe and Japan started it in China, there was great consternation when Americans discovered that the French tiger was made of paper and that the British Navy could not sail up the Rhine. Further, Japan's aggression in the Far East seemed a clear warning to the United States.

As Rear Admiral Samuel Eliot Morison, the distinguished naval historian of World War II, sagely put it in *The Two-Ocean War: A Short History of the United States Navy in the Second World War* (Boston: Little, Brown, 1963), in 1939–41 Americans wanted only to be let alone; seeking neither world power nor world responsibility, they ironically found power and responsibility thrust upon them by Germany and Japan, nations that avidly desired both. (And, to compound historical irony, nations that today are among our staunchest allies.)

After Pearl Harbor those Americans who wanted to stay out of international affairs and those who wanted to aid beleaguered Britain in her fight against Germany didn't really have anything to quarrel about any more. For Japan, in its sneak attack, took care of that by making the United States a nation at war. President Roosevelt's declaration of war against Japan on Monday, December 8, was a mere formality that had the hearty approval of everyone. And then Germany declared war on the United States.

British historian A. J. P. Taylor has raised an interesting "what if" question:

> The mind boggles at the speculation of what would have happened if Hitler had delayed his declaration of war against the United States for even a few weeks: by then the Americans would have been involved in the Pacific and turned their backs on Europe. Hitler never considered this course seriously. . . . The very unscrupulousness of the Japanese action appealed to him.*

At times it appears that a definition of war should involve a quest for heroes and scapegoats. Although there were plenty of heroes

---

* *The Second World War: An Illustrated History* (New York: G. P. Putnam's Sons, 1975)

around Oahu on the morning of December 8, the American public seemed to be more interested in scapegoats.

The sneak attack on Pearl Harbor became the most thoroughly investigated military action that ever involved American arms; millions of words have been written about it. Heads rolled. General Short and Admiral Kimmel were sent into retirement; several incompetent officers were eventually shuffled to posts where they could do little damage to the war effort. Today it appears that not enough blame was put on high rankers in Washington who did not make the threat of attack sufficiently clear to the commanders on the hot points. Nearly everybody came under criticism, but it was the commanders on the scene whose careers were destroyed.

Even President Roosevelt was blamed in a paranoid attack by some of his political enemies who claimed that he had encouraged unpreparedness at Pearl Harbor—even that he was willing to sacrifice half his navy just to involve the nation in war on the side of Britain. If that was Roosevelt's plot, then he had as co-conspirators some of the greatest patriots the country ever has known, including two sterling members of the Republican Party, Secretary of War Henry L. Stimson and Secretary of the Navy Frank Knox.

It is impossible to finger specific inividuals for blame over the state of apathy and unpreparedness at Pearl Harbor. Most of the blame must be placed on a general state of mind in the American people, as reflected in their armed forces.

The feeling of officers and men after years of being put on the alert against false alarms has been well described by the historical writer Edwin P. Hoyt as being "like the reaction of the townspeople in the fable of the little boy who cried wolf."* Hoyt quotes an unnamed officer of the Pacific Fleet in those days as saying, "All those scares got to be ridiculous and people thought, 'Oh, thunder, here's

---

* *How They Won the War in the Pacific* (New York: Weybright and Talley, 1970)

another one of these. . . . we won't pay any attention. . . .' "

Whoever was to blame, a good deal of hysteria remained loose in the country after the event. One of the worst examples was the way law-abiding Japanese-Americans on the west coast were herded into concentration camps. Though the camps were not like those of the Germans, it was a situation that echoed Nazi Germany. At first there was much hysterical fear in Hawaii, too, where many people anticipated sabotage and destruction by some of the 150,000 persons of Japanese descent then in the islands. The fears were unfounded; there never was a single instance of sabotage by resident Japanese in Hawaii.

If saboteurs had wanted to cripple the war effort in the Pacific, they had an extraordinary target in the Pearl Harbor tank farms. Stored there were 4,500,000 barrels of fuel oil. Historians will always wonder why Yamamoto did not choose to make the American fuel supplies, instead of the battleships, the principal target along with the planes on the airfields. The battleships were old and outmoded for the new kind of naval warfare that was going to be fought. (They could make no better than 21 knots, whereas the carriers could make up to 34; thus they could not operate together.) Without that precious fuel the fleet would have been immobilized for months—some have estimated for as long as a year. Furthermore, the Americans were desperately short of tankers in the Pacific. Japanese intelligence knew this, and its officers must have seen that their strong submarine force could have been highly effective in blocking transportation of vital fuel to Hawaii. Possibly Yamamoto and his planners decided to go after the battleships instead of the fuel supplies because they represented a more dramatic target which, if destroyed, would impress the world with Japan's power. For, great as was Yamamoto's personal faith in the strength of seaborne aircraft, prior to the attack on Pearl Harbor the battleship still was king.

There were two basic realities behind American involvement in a Pacific war: the decline of China and the rise of Japan.

Since the turn of the century the United States had been trying to aid China by urging Japan and the European powers to keep hands off the weak giant. But Japan became increasingly aggressive. After defeating Russia in the War of 1904–05 and obtaining Korea and a sphere of influence in Manchuria, the Japanese slowly munched their way into mainland China. In 1937 they took Shanghai and Nanking and the next year seized Hankow and Canton, thus controlling the entire China coast.

Chiang Kai-shek, China's leader, withdrew the seat of his weak and corrupt government to inland Chungking. There he continued to receive American aid by way of the Burma Road and through the ports of French Indo China.

The Japanese, in their hunger for empire, became involved in war with Russia. In July 1938 and again in May 1939 they took the offensive against the Russians from bases in Manchuria. Both times they were so soundly beaten that they lost their taste for Russian territory. They had long coveted the raw materials of Malaya and the Indies, especially oil, and saw an opportunity to move south after the colonial powers in that area—Britain, France and the Netherlands —became involved in war in Europe.

On September 27, 1940, Japan, Germany and Italy signed the Tripartite Pact, in which each promised to enter into war if any of the three was attacked by a new enemy. Through this pact Hitler hoped to beef up Japan's confidence to the point of making war against the United States and thereby divert American strength into the Pacific and away from Europe. Around that same time Japan persuaded the French to let her air force operate from northern Indo-China. Then, in July 1941 Japan presented France with an ultimatum demanding the use of air bases throughout Indochina. This move put the Japanese almost at the gates of Singapore, the British bastion in Malaya.

Roosevelt reacted by freezing Japanese assets, thereby halting the supply of oil to Japan. Only by such strong measures, he believed, could the Japanese be persuaded to halt their aggression. The British and Dutch followed the American lead. In this manner Japan lost three-fourths of her foreign trade, and nine-tenths of her oil supply was cut off. Japanese leaders believed that if they did not break the embargo the nation's economy would collapse by the spring of 1942.

4

Two Admirals

On November 28, 1941, an American task force filed out of the serene waters of Pearl Harbor to engage in a training exercise. It was commanded by Vice Admiral William F. Halsey, Jr., aboard the aircraft carrier *Enterprise* and included three battleships, four heavy cruisers and a screening group of destroyers. Once they were clear of the channel, Halsey split his force in two. One section, designated Task Force 8, comprised *Enterprise,* three heavy cruisers and nine destroyers. The other, comprising the battleships, one cruiser and the remaining destroyers, Halsey designated Task Force 2 under the command of Rear Admiral Milo F. Draemel, whom he ordered to carry out training exercises off the coast of Oahu. Then Halsey, maintaining radio silence and sending all messages by flag or blinker signal, shaped course for the west.

The commander of Halsey's screening force of three cruisers and nine destroyers was his friend of many years Rear Admiral Raymond A. Spruance. Spruance had no idea where Bill Halsey was leading them, and he would no more have thought of inquiring where than he would have resigned from the Navy. It would have been difficult to find two men more unlike and yet so compatible as Halsey and Spruance. Halsey was then 59 and originally from Elizabeth, New Jersey. Spruance, 55, had been born in Baltimore, Maryland. Both had shared similar experiences in the slow and often frustrating climb of Navy career officers. Recollections of their childhoods underscore the great differences in the natures of these good friends.

Bill Halsey, once known as Pudge and before that as Willie, wore long yellow curls as an infant. Once when he was two word came to his New Jersey home that his naval lieutenant father was returning on leave. Willie, as excited as his mother by the news, raced around the house with her trying to set things straight. But he only managed to knock over things.

Many years later Halsey's sister Deborah recalled, "He was always like that. He would walk into any room and immediately everything was disarranged—furniture, ashtrays all pushed around. But we never minded the disorder. He made the place alive and exciting. In later years, whenever he arrived, a dozen people would somehow learn about it and trail along, and soon the house would be filled."*

Willie Halsey grew up to be outgoing, but not boisterous; gentle to his friends and tough to his enemies; ever warm, yet always welcoming a fight. Once, when Willie came home with a bleeding scalp, his alarmed mother wanted to know what had happened. He said a kid had hit him with a baseball bat. Mrs. Halsey wanted to see the boy's mother about it, but Willie told her: "Never mind, I'll take care of that guy myself."

Raymond Ames Spruance, named after an illustrious Methodist missionary bishop ancestor, did not grow up a scrapper like Willie Halsey. While there was warmth in the Halsey family, there was coldness in the Spruances'. Raymond's father was aloof, his mother

---

* *William F. Halsey: Fighting Admiral* by Chandler Whipple (New York: G. P. Putnam's Sons, 1968)

involved with personal ambitions. Spruance grew up a lonely child, shy and withdrawn, who was raised mainly by his grandmother and three maiden aunts.

A boyhood friend recalled that Spruance "was neither a leader nor an active participant in the boisterous running and shouting games that took place in the dusty schoolyard before school or at recess times. He always came to school with a neighbor boy who was a classmate and somewhat more robust, so that it sometimes seemed to me that Raymond rather avoided independence of action."*

Spruance was a good student, Halsey a poor one. Indeed, Halsey probably would not have won an appointment to the Naval Academy if his mother had not become such a vociferous Washington lobbyist in his behalf that some officials hid in their offices when they heard she was coming.

As usual, Bill Halsey did all possible to help his own cause. On January 26, 1897, he wrote President William McKinley, addressing him by his Civil War title of "Major," which seemed much more impressive to the military-minded 14-year-old than the mere civilian office of president of the United States. In the letter extolling his ability to become a great naval officer Bill Halsey misspelled the name of the Secretary of the Navy and described himself as a "border" (*sic*) at Swarthmore Grammar. In spite of his letter and other tactical errors, Halsey eventually obtained an appointment to the academy. More important, he managed to graduate—albeit forty-third of 62 in the class of 1904.

Spruance, on the other hand, made outstanding scores in his entrance exams to the academy and stood twenty-fifth in a class of 209 when he was graduated in 1906. In his excellent biography of Spruance, *The Quiet Warrior,* Thomas B. Buell, a naval officer himself, writes:

---

* *The Quiet Warrior: A Biography of Admiral Raymond A. Spruance* by Thomas B. Buell(Boston: Little, Brown, 1974)

Spruance was a classic intellectual in the sense that he was extremely rational and relied upon his intellect rather than his emotions or feelings. He regarded the war against Japan as in intellectual exercise that posed a complex yet interesting series of problems that challenged and stimulated his mind. Those problems had to be solved using logic and reason that was unaffected by the violent passions of war.

Spruance, reserved and intellectual, and Halsey, outgoing and emotional, became fast friends—as did their wives. Each respected in the other qualities he felt he himself lacked.

Spruance's intellectual bent made him like any work that stimulated his mind. Thus he became an expert in electrical engineering, involving himself with such things as developing new gunnery fire control systems. His expertise in this led him into specialist's duties that, to his great distress, kept him out of combat in World War I. Halsey, on the other hand, found what he wanted during that war as a destroyer officer in convoy duties against warring German submarines.

The friendship between the two was formed in the 1920s when Spruance took command of a ship in Halsey's destroyer division and came under the influence of his senior's skillful, exhilarating leadership. Then it was that the accomplished, aggressive deck officer Halsey first took the measure of his quiet junior. He found Spruance a calm man who never lost his composure under the most trying experiences. Spruance was fair, tolerant, wise, confident; his officers and men responded in kind to the respect and loyalty he showed them. The shy child raised by maiden aunts had grown into a master mariner who was a fine leader of men.

One day when Spruance's destroyer was anchored in the French North African port of Bizerte his alarmed deck officer dashed to him and said, "Captain, we just dropped a depth charge over the stern!" If the French found out, they could raise enough trouble to damage Spruance's career.

But he remained unperturbed. "Well," he told the officer calmly, "pick it up and put it back."

Spruance attended the Naval War College in Newport, Rhode Island, in 1926 and returned in the 1930s for two tours of duty as a staff officer. An important part of the curriculum was elaborate war games played on a large board in which opposing fleets fought theoretical sea battles. Spruance excelled at war games. Japan was conceived as America's most likely enemy in another war, and it was believed the Japanese would start it with a surprise attack, as they had begun their war against Russia early in the century.

The naval thinking at the time was that the outcome of a war would be decided by the big guns of battleships. Submarines were conceived to be only scouting vessels, too vulnerable to maneuver with the fleet. Carrier aviation was just beginning; it was considered to be a supplement to but never a replacement for the battleship. Many important aspects of a projected war against Japan were ignored. For instance, the United States would need island bases to advance across the Pacific, but few at the War College gave much thought to training in the amphibious warfare necessary to capture islands. Another widely ignored subject was the vital one of logistics: methods of supplying fuel, food and ammunition to ships operating in distant waters.

From the advantage of later time it appears that the War College of the 1920s and 1930s was not doing a very good job of preparing its officer students for the war they would fight in the 1940s. But it did teach them the basic strategy in a war against Japan. Spruance enjoyed the lively intellectual atmosphere of the College. And it was natural that a bright, ambitious officer like him should seek service with the battleships which were at the heart of naval plans for the future.

Probably it was natural, too, that a more restless spirit like Halsey's took happily to naval aviation. In 1934 Rear Admiral Ernest J. King, Chief of the Bureau of Aeronautics, offered Captain William F. Halsey command of the powerful new aircraft carrier *Saratoga* if he could pass the aviation observer's course at Pensacola, which would not require his passing the difficult pilot's eye test. Halsey, 51 and a grandfather, leaped at the chance, to the distress of his wife Frances.*

After a few days of flying around Pensacola as an observer, Halsey decided he wanted to become a student pilot. If he was going to command a carrier, he wanted to know the problems pilots faced— what they thought and how they reacted to various conditions. This feeling of Halsey's for others gave his pilots and subordinates undying loyalty to him during his years of high command in the Pacific war.

Halsey, the oldest and highest-ranking student at Pensacola in 1934, pulled enough weight that people "forgot" to give him an eye exam, and he started pilot training. Sometimes shaky on landings, he once ground-looped and another time did a front flip. Once when he couldn't read the compass because of his poor eyesight, he followed a railroad track, turned off on a wrong branch of the line and had everybody at the base worried to death about him until he buzzed back. After that he had corrective lenses put in his flying goggles, but corrective lenses were no help for the deafness that sometimes made it hard for him to understand radio communications.

Nevertheless, Bill Halsey became a pilot and had logged more than 1,100 flying hours by that November 28, 1941, when he and Spruance sailed west from Pearl Harbor together as Task Force 8.

Once Task Force 8 was out of sight of land, Halsey signalled Spruance's screening force from *Enterprise* to arm for battle, sink any Japanese ships sighted and shoot down any Japanese planes. Whatever the nation's state of preparedness, Bill Halsey was ready to fight a war. Spruance still didn't know where they were going. As usual, Halsey was closemouthed. He was the one who made the decisions; Spruance's

* *Admiral Halsey's Story* by Fleet Admiral William F. Halsey and J. Bryan III (New York: Whittlesey House, 1947)

function was simply to make his ships responsive to Halsey's orders.

Eventually he learned that the task force's mission was to deliver a dozen Marine fighters to Wake Island. The plan was Admiral Kimmel's reaction to the November 27 warning from Washington over the threat of war. For weeks now Kimmel had chosen to concentrate on training rather than constant vigilance, which would have exhausted his men and used up valuable materiel. Even after the November 27 warning he did not switch the fleet at Pearl Harbor to a full alert.

Spruance, like Halsey, believed war was close upon them. In his quiet way he awaited it fatalistically. After promotion to Rear Admiral he had hoped for a battleship division command. Instead, in September 1941 at Pearl Harbor, he had raised his flag on *Northampton* as commander of Cruiser Division 5, comprising four heavy cruisers.

These ships were not comfortable. At high speeds they vibrated badly. At low speeds they rolled sickeningly. They were poorly ventilated and somewhat leaky. Though side portholes could be opened for fresh air, they usually shipped water when the vessels were underway. Thus they became intolerably hot when battened down for General Quarters. They were armed with powerful eight-inch guns, but had been stripped of their torpedo tubes and did not have effective antiaircraft armament. All flammable and superflous material had been removed, but owing to design limitations imposed by prewar naval disarmament treaties, these cruisers still were not ready to fight a resourceful enemy.

Spruance made himself at ease on *Northampton* despite her discomforts. He had an efficient staff that handled details, and weeks before he had issued careful orders for battle readiness by the division if war began. As was his custom at sea, he kept to himself. He slept remarkably long hours, read omnivorously and every day, when weather permitted, walked the decks for miles. At age 55 the graying Spruance was lean and fit from long devotion to regular exercise and a spare diet.

The task force continued west until *Enterprise* sent off the Marine planes near Wake, then turned back for Pearl. Halsey planned to enter the harbor on December 6, but progress was slowed by the need to refuel the destroyers in a heavy sea. Arrival time at Pearl was postponed to December 7. Spruance was disappointed, for he had asked his wife, Margaret, to meet him for dinner on Saturday evening after his ship docked. (She and their daughter, also named Margaret, had come to Hawaii with him in September.)

On Sunday morning, December 7, the task force was 200 miles west of Pearl and Spruance was in his cabin when his flag secretary phoned from the bridge and tensely reported the message Bellinger had just sent from Pearl Harbor:

AIR RAID, PEARL HARBOR—THIS IS NOT A DRILL.

"Thank you." Spruance never had sounded calmer. "You know what to do."

Thus the flag secretary put in force the battle readiness orders Spruance had issued long before. Immediately the admiral went to the bridge and remained there for the next twenty-four hours. At first no one could believe it actually had happened. But soon it became clear it really had. The air waves were an excited jumble of conflicting messages. The attacking Japanese fleet was imagined to be hither, thither and yonder. Halsey was in a frustrated rage over which direction to sail in search of the enemy. As the day wore on, other American vessels appeared and joined Task Force 8.

The one solid radar sighting of the Japanese fleet on Oahu was somehow misread in that day of chaos, and Task Force 8 was told the enemy was stealing away to the southwest. Halsey and Spruance went charging off in that direction while the Japanese were withdrawing to the northwest. They never did glimpse a Japanese plane or ship in all their voyage to Wake and back.

Spruance never revealed his thoughts during those hours of tension and frustration after the attack, but it is safe to assume that—like all men of fighting age on that day—he thought much about his family. The Spruances' son, Edward, was a lieutenant aboard the submarine *Tambor* based at Pearl Harbor. The admiral had been a stern, strict parent against whose authority Edward often had rebelled. Now, as the task force prowled the Pacific wastes, Spruance must have worried about Edward as well as his wife and young Margaret. How had they fared in the attack?

Perhaps, too, he had time to reflect on how fortunate it was for the nation that the only three aircraft carriers in the Pacific Fleet were gone from Pearl Harbor. While *Enterprise* was on her mission to Wake, Kimmel had sent another task force built around the carrier *Lexington* to deliver 25 bombers to Midway Island, and the third carrier, *Saratoga*, had left Pearl for the West Coast.

Task Force 8's wild goose chase to the southwest used up precious fuel, and Spruance notified Halsey it was imperative his destroyers return to Pearl before they went dry. Around noon on Monday, December 8, the force filed slowly into Pearl. The devastation there stunned Spruance and Halsey, along with all the men in their force. Buell writes in *The Quiet Warrior:*

When Spruance reached home, his self-control dissolved. His wife and daughter were shocked—Spruance was a broken man. The three sat at a table, and he began to tell them what he had seen and felt. His voice choked with emotion, tears wetted his face, and he could scarcely speak. Yet he forced himself to talk about his shock and his grief, as though talking would purge his agony and suffering. Never before and never again would his wife and daughter see him in such despair. The destruction at Pearl Harbor was the most shattering experience of his life.

5

CINPAC

A week after the attack on Pearl Harbor Secretary of the Navy Knox called in Rear Admiral Chester W. Nimitz, Chief of the Bureau of Navigation, and asked him, "How soon can you be ready to travel?"

Nimitz said that depended on where he was going and how long he'd be away.

"You're going to take command of the Pacific Fleet," Knox told him, "and I think you're going to be gone a long time."*

A few days later Nimitz took a train to the West Coast and flew on to Pearl Harbor. There he was greeted by Kimmel, the friend and Annapolis classmate he would replace as Commander in Chief of the Pacific Fleet (CINCPAC).

President Roosevelt admired both Nimitz and Kimmel. Many months before the Pearl Harbor attack he had offered command of the Pacific Fleet to Nimitz, who refused because it would have meant his being advanced over the heads of nearly forty seniors who would have been made jealous by his promotion. Roosevelt next offered the

* *Nimitz* by E. B. Potter (Annapolis: Naval Institute Press, 1976)

command to Kimmel, who leaped at the opportunity. If Nimitz had accepted the offer the first time, it well might have been his career rather than Kimmel's which was destroyed.

Nimitz, a genial, ruddy man whose sandy hair was turning white, had great feeling for others. He had deep sympathy with Kimmel, who was portly, formal-mannered and highly capable. If Kimmel had kept the fleet at full alert, as some civilian critics later suggested he should have done, his men would have been too exhausted to fight well when the attack came. His decision to concentrate on training at the expense of alertness and his interpretation of the warnings he received were perfectly understandable to many of his fellow officers.

When Nimitz arrived at Pearl Harbor he was dismayed to see how aged and shaken Kimmel was from his experience. Kimmel had been staring out a window on December 7 with a numbed feeling, watching the destruction of his fleet—and his good reputation—when a spent .50-caliber bullet crashed through the window and struck his breast. "Too bad it didn't kill me," he said.

In picking Nimitz to resurrect the Pacific Fleet, the President and Secretary of the Navy had selected an officer with an excellent record for innovation and efficiency. As chief of the Bureau of Navigation he had been a director of officer personnel, trying to fit the right man into the right job. Before that he had been outstanding in the submarine service. His research had helped the development of diesel engines for submarines, and in 1920 he had been the chief architect of the submarine base at Pearl Harbor. Six years later he was among the founders of the Naval Reserve Officer Training Corps. In every naval activity he had undertaken Nimitz had immersed himself deeply. As he put it more than once in interviews, "You always play to win."

The new CINCPAC was 56 years old, a native of Fredericksburg, Texas, and had graduated from the academy seventh in a class of 114. Like Spruance, Nimitz was a great advocate of physical fitness. Unlike Spruance, he genuinely enjoyed the company of others. Nimitz was fond of tennis, swimming, hiking, cribbage, pitching horseshoes, classical music. When tensions of command built up, he often worked them off on the pistol range, where he was a crack shot.

Upon Nimitz's broad shoulders was placed the heaviest responsibilities ever undertaken by an American naval officer: to rebuild a huge fleet and put it on the offensive against Japan. Aware of the great weight of the job, he said, "I'll be lucky to last six months. The public may demand action and results faster than I can produce." He would have much preferred any kind of combat command. But once appointed to his office of complex responsibilities he took on the burdens with remarkable cheerfulness.

Nimitz, who would be boss of hundreds of thousands of men, had in turn one of the toughest bosses ever. He was Commander in Chief U.S. Fleet Admiral Ernest J. King (known as COMINCH), the man Roosevelt and Knox had named to replace Stark. King was reputedly so tough that he shaved with a blowtorch. Such a man is never beloved; indeed, some said that King had more enemies in the U.S. Navy than in the Japanese. At age 63 he had the demeanor of an eagle and possessed all an eagle's prowess and ruthlessness.

E. B. Potter, a professor of history at the U.S. Naval Academy, writes in his notable biography, *Nimitz:*

> Although their styles were in sharp contrast, King and Nimitz were more alike than different. Simplicity and directness were the keynotes of their characters. They were both dedicated to their country and to the Navy, though King's interests were more narrowly naval. Both were men of integrity and keen intelligence, and both were born strategists and organizers, with a genius for clarifying and simplifying and a jaundiced eye for useless complications and waste motions. Their chief difference lay in their attitudes toward their fellow human beings. King had little of Nimitz's understanding of, and empathy for, people.

Nimitz took on his staggering command problems in the midst of a revolution in naval tactics and strategy. When he had studied at the Naval War College the battleship was supreme, but the successful attack on Pearl had changed that: now the carrier was king.

However, in carrier operations alone, to say nothing of the many other naval efforts, scores of corrections were essential if ships were to fight effectively. There were not enough oilers for necessary refueling of carriers at sea. Something was wrong with torpedoes, plane as well as submarine; they had a tendency to go off course or not detonate. Carriers needed more fighter planes for protection. There were nowhere near enough plane crew replacements or aircraft mechanics. The slow Devastator torpedo bombers needed to be replaced by the faster Avengers. The fogging of windshields, sights and night telescopes in the dive bombers had to be corrected. Torpedo and bombing attacks had to be more closely coordinated. Every carrier needed two long-range radar sets. The 1000-pound bomb was erratic, the bomb-release solenoids unreliable. Indeed, the whole range of bombs and torpedoes had to be improved if the Navy ever hoped to achieve a decisive victory.

Meanwhile, disaster after disaster befell the Allies on both fronts. In the Atlantic, German submarines were sinking Allied ships faster than they could be replaced. In the Middle East, the tanks of the brilliant German Field Marshal Erwin Rommel were chewing up the British, who lost control of the Mediterranean—though not because of Rommel. At the same time other German armies advanced victoriously eastward against the Russians. Still, the worst Allied debacle was in the western Pacific, where the Japanese swept everything before them.

American and British plans for fighting Japan in the western Pacific were based on the idea of preserving two strongholds, the cities of Manila and Singapore. But maintaining each depended on its being reinforced.

The commander of American and Filipino forces, with headquarters in Manila, was General Douglas MacArthur, a former U. S. Army Chief of Staff, who was 61 at the outbreak of war. The American plan, conceived years before, was for MacArthur to hang on at Manila until the American fleet sailed from Pearl Harbor and helped him throw back an enemy invasion. However, as things have a way of happening in war, it didn't turn out as planned.

First the fleet was immobilized by the attack on Pearl, then matters went wrong at Manila. MacArthur aimed to frustrate an attack on the Philippines by deploying his B-17 Flying Fortresses against the Japanese air and naval bases on Formosa. Why that didn't happen still is obscured by a cloud of controversy. Manila was alerted the moment of the attack on Pearl Harbor. Morison says the Flying Fortresses didn't get off because of quarreling among MacArthur's air officers. In any event, nine hours after the first warning the Japanese attacked Manila and destroyed half of MacArthur's air force on the ground. Having gained control of the air over the Philippines, they smashed ground and sea forces in the area at will.

A Japanese force attacked the British base of Hong Kong on December 8 and completed the victory on Christmas, taking 12,000 prisoners at a cost of less than 3,000 casualties. The Japanese performance on the Malay Peninsula was similar to what they did in the Philippines. First they established control of the air. If the British were to defend Singapore they must prevent enemy landings to the north on the peninsula. This they failed to do. British Admiral Tom Phillips, who still believed that battleships did not need air cover, took two of Britain's finest—*Prince of Wales* and battle cruiser *Repulse* —north to try to break up Japanese landings. He had no air cover. Japanese bombers and torpedo planes sank both ships with a loss of only three aircraft. The chief British fortifications at Singapore were on its seaward side, but it was vulnerable through its back door. None knew this better than the Japanese. They captured the place in mid-

February with a force of 35,000 and made prisoners of its 80,000 defenders.

"It was," writes Taylor, "the greatest capitulation in British history and one of its most discreditable."

The Japanese juggernaut rolled on. Burma fell, the British abandoning it as indefensible. Early in January the first Japanese landed in the Dutch East Indies and followed their custom of sweeping ahead quickly. At the end of February the Dutch Rear Admiral Karel Doorman, who commanded all Allied naval forces in Southeast Asia, assembled all available American, British and Dutch warships to attack Japanese convoys. The force comprised two heavy cruisers, three light cruisers and nine destroyers. It had difficulties in communications, but its chief lack was an air scouting force. Literally a fleet without eyes, it paid the price for its weaknesses. In what became known as the Battle of the Java Sea. Doorman lost half his force. The remainder were scattered and eventually destroyed.

That ended resistance in Indonesia. About 98,000 Dutch East Indian troops became captives when the Dutch surrendered on March 8.

Three days later Roosevelt ordered MacArthur to leave the Philippines. By that time the core of American ground forces, without sea or air power, had been penned up on Corregidor, the fortified island in Manila Bay, and the nearby Bataan Peninsula. MacArthur escaped to Australia by torpedo boat and airplane, saying, "I shall return," and leaving to subordinates the distasteful task of surrendering.

There was no alternative to surrender. The American and Filipino defenders could not be resupplied or reinforced by sea or air. The inevitable occurred on May 6. The Americans and Filipinos lost about 140,000 dead or imprisoned. Japanese casualties amounted to only about 12,000. Never before had the United States surrendered so much to a foreign enemy. The effect at home, however, was much like that following the sneak attack on Pearl Harbor: Instead of despairing, most Americans were united in a determination to turn defeat into eventual victory.

The amazing thing was that the Japanese achieved their victories with relatively small ground forces, usually smaller than their opponents. Their method was first to establish dominance of the air and then to use their highly mobile sea, air and ground power to move swiftly against their targets. Throughout the war the Japanese Army never engaged the mass of its strength against the Americans in the Pacific. The bulk of the army remained in Manchuria and China while the Japanese depended mainly on their sea-air power to take and hold their Pacific island empire.

Douglas MacArthur hoped to be the sole organizer of the Allied offensive in the Pacific, but that was not to be. On March 30 the Joint Chiefs revealed their plan. MacArthur would be Supreme Commander, Allied Forces in the Southwest Pacific Area, which included Australia, the Solomon Islands, the Bismarcks, New Guinea and the Philippines. Nimitz was named Commander in Chief Pacific Ocean Area (CINCPOA), comprising all the rest of the Pacific except for some shipping lanes off Latin America. Thus he wore two hats. As CINCPAC he commanded the Pacific Fleet. As CINCPOA he was in command of all American and Allied land, sea and air forces in his area.

The United States generally followed a "Germany First" policy that gave a higher priority of men and materiel for the European theater than for the Pacific. Not all the war chiefs agreed on this plan at all times. King, for example, always advocated increased priority to the Pacific theater and sometimes was a powerful persuader with his fellow leaders.

The situation was as bleak in the Central Pacific as in the western waters. Guam fell, Wake was captured after its doughty defenders beat back one invasion force. Everywhere Japan retained the initiative. Nimitz's forces could only react, which is quite different from attack.

Thus, when it was feared the Japanese would take Samoa and

cut the vital lifeline connecting Hawaii and the United States with Australia, a force of marines was sent from San Diego to bolster the defenses on Samoa. The Marine convoy, shepherded by a task force grouped around the carrier *Yorktown* and commanded by Rear Admiral Frank Jack Fletcher, sailed early in January. Nimitz ordered Halsey in carrier *Enterprise* and Spruance with his screening cruisers and destroyers to rendezvous with Fletcher. After the marines were landed safely in Samoa the carrier groups were to steam north into the Gilbert and Marshall Islands to raid Japanese bases.

King had put the pressure on Nimitz to begin raids at once. In theory the purpose was to weaken the Japanese and gain information about their bases. In practicality the aim was to give the Americans combat experience and boost morale at home by showing that the U. S. Navy still was alive and fighting in the Pacific. But in truth such rambling expeditions served little military purpose.

There was one overriding problem among the many Nimitz faced as CINCPAC. He was looking for fighting admirals as avidly as President Lincoln once had hunted capable generals to pit against the military genius of the Confederacy.

Halsey was the outstanding example of the kind of daring fighter Nimitz was seeking. Halsey, said Nimitz, "has that rare combination of intellectual capacity and military audacity, and one who can calculate to a cat's whisker the risks involved." Halsey, someone said, handled an aircraft carrier with a classy style that made it look like a maneuvering destroyer—almost like a speedboat.

While Nimitz quickly saw Halsey's capabilities, he as yet did not know how the old line "battleship admirals" such as Spruance would adapt to the new style of carrier warfare. The hit-run raids into the islands would reveal something about Spruance as well as Halsey, both undergoing their World War II baptism of fire. Nimitz left it up to Halsey to select the targets. At the time American intelligence knew almost nothing about the Marshalls, which Japan had possessed for the past twenty years while forbidding all foreign visitors. Recently the

Japanese had seized the Gilberts from the British and presumably were busily fortifying some of them. Halsey decided *Enterprise* planes would hit Wotje and three other atolls in the northern Marshalls. Simultaneously Spruance would bombard Wotje with two cruisers and a destroyer. Meantime Fletcher with *Yorktown* would strike three other island targets.

Spruance prepared his battle plans carefully—more carefully than Halsey, it appears. After thirty-nine years of naval service he was finally going into combat for the first time, and he wanted matters to proceed well. They did not. To Spruance's angry disappointment his cruisers' antiaircraft fire was ineffective and a false submarine scare wrecked both his bombardment plan and his division's discipline. He felt the mission a failure.

At one point in the proceedings his young flag lieutenant, William M. McCormick, protested his Admiral's standing out on the open bridge, saying, "Don't you think you'd better get back in the conning tower?"

"No," replied Spruance, "but maybe you'd better because you have so much longer to live than I have."

Halsey seemed to have a very good time during the excitement. He launched and recovered numerous air strikes while maneuvering *Enterprise* around Wotje for nine hours before deciding it was time to get out of there while Japanese planes still were looking for him. Thereupon he announced the formation of a club that became legendary to its fighting members and was called "Haul Ass With Halsey." He and Spruance with their ships returned to a hero's welcome at Pearl Harbor. Whistles blared, bells clanged and thousands cheered over the success of the great raid.

Halsey was, of course, the returning hero. Scarcely anyone even knew Spruance's name. Which suited Spruance fine. There never was a man cherished privacy more than Raymond A. Spruance. He was happy that his old friend Bill Halsey had become a hero—just as long as none of the notoriety rubbed off on him.

One can imagine Spruance saying to intimate friends that the raid really had accomplished nothing. One also can imagine Halsey saying that of course it had, the raid had given the American people a much-needed shot in the arm at a bad time. One thing the raid did for sure was to give the American public a new naval hero in a war remarkably lacking in heroes. And the hero's name was not Raymond A. Spruance.

King kept pressure on Nimitz for more raids. So, on February 11, Nimitz ordered Halsey and Spruance to hit recently captured Wake Island. Except as a training exercise, the raid served no good military purpose. Everyone knew it—everyone, that is, except the American public, which was famished for favorable news about American arms.

News correspondents rode along on *Enterprise* with Halsey, who charmed them with salty conversation. They were awed by the dust his planes and Spruance's guns raised on Wake, and the stories they filed made the expedition sound like a great American victory. If nothing else, it established Halsey as the kind of sea-dog hero land-lubbers had admired since the Elizabethan days of Drake and Hawkins. His public nickname of "Bull" came about as a transmission typographical error in a news story for his Navy nickname of "Bill." No one in the Navy ever thought of calling him "Bull." But the name, evoking an image of a bull in a china shop, delighted the public. Back home bumper stickers began to urge "Bull On With Halsey" for those too prim to paste on the already popular sticker "Haul Ass With Halsey."

There is no reason to sound patronizing about the public emotions of those days, for the war could not have been won on the fighting fronts without full cooperation on the home front. Civilians had to make the planes, ships, guns and hundreds of other things the fighters needed. No one knew better than Chester Nimitz that victory would come only from the most careful planning, that battles are almost invariably decided by superior weight of men and materiel, that successful military effort is chiefly the intelligent placement in the field of a successful industrial effort at home.

The next spectacular the Pacific stage managers thought up for the folks at home was really a wow.

In March the Joint Chiefs of Staff decided it would be great for morale to bomb Tokyo in a cooperative display of Army-Navy fireworks. (There was, of course, no separate Air Force until after the war.) The expedition would be commanded by Halsey, naturally, and would be grouped around *Enterprise* and another carrier which would join the Pacific Fleet, *Hornet*. Aboard *Hornet* were 16 Army Air Force B-25 bombers commanded by Lieutenant Colonel James H. Doolittle. With luck these bombers could manage to take off from an aircraft carrier, but the flight deck was too short for them to land. So, after being launched from *Hornet* off the coast of Japan, they would have to fly 1,100 miles beyond Tokyo and land on friendly Chinese airfields.

Spruance, in command of the expedition's cruiser screen, fumed openly at the idea of the raid. He told anyone who would listen that it was ridiculous to divert two precious carriers of the four in the Pacific, and so many cruisers and destroyers from the main scene of Japanese operations in the Southwest Pacific, and endanger them in a raid against the Japanese homeland that served no worthy military purpose. Halsey and Nimitz agreed with his estimate of the situation, but there was no sense in trying to argue with King and the Joint Chiefs once they had made up their minds. And the revered Joint Chiefs were far from being a bunch of military fools. They understood what the weak Pacific Fleet could do—and what it could not. They understood the need for popular support of the war effort and, since that was all they could hope to achieve in the Pacific at the moment, that was what they ordered undertaken.

Nevertheless, Spruance continued to express his annoyance privately. In a letter written around that time to his wife Margaret, who had returned to California with their daughter, he said:

> The thing I don't like about our press is the constant over-emphasis they give to comparatively unimportant events, with the result that the public gets a wrong picture of how things are really going. Then the public indulges in wishful thinking. I like the way Winston Churchill does not hesitate to tell the British when things are going badly.*

The Tokyo raid task force hoped to launch its B-25s about 500 miles from Tokyo. But early on the morning of April 18 the force was sighted by Japanese fishing vessels which immediately radioed reports of their presence. It was decided to launch the bombers at once, even though they were nearly 700 miles from Tokyo. One by one the B-25s lumbered along the deck of *Hornet* and climbed into a gray sky.

Despite the fishing boats' report on the task force, Doolittle's raiders took Tokyo completely by surprise. They did little damage to the city, but they greatly amazed the Japanese people, who had been led to believe from government propaganda that the Americans had been virtually knocked out of the war. They also hit a few other cities. None of the American planes was shot down over Japan, but some pilots had to ditch off the coast or crash-land in China. Two were picked up by the Japanese and executed. (This was a crime for which the Japanese responsible were executed by the Americans after the war.)

President Roosevelt announced the Tokyo raid in a radio broadcast, and Americans everywhere were thrilled and delighted.

---

* *The Quiet Warrior.*

6

The Codebreakers

The United States probably would have won the war against Japan without the codebreakers. But it would have been much more difficult.

Everything to do with American breaking of Japanese codes since the beginning of the effort in the 1920s has been classified Top Secret by the U. S. Government. But enough information has appeared in print to give a clear notion of the operations. Thorough studies of codebreaking in the Pacific during World War II are offered by Potter in *Nimitz* and in an absorbing history, *Silent Victory: The U. S. Submarine War Against Japan* by Clay Blair, Jr. (Philadelphia and New York: J. B. Lippincott, 1975).

One of the first of America's great cryptographers was a man named Herbert O. Yardley, who headed the Army's codebreaking organization in World War I. After the war he prevailed on the Army, the Navy and the State Department to support his codebreaking efforts in what became known as the Black Chamber, located in New York City. There he and a few assistants began to break Japanese diplomatic codes. By the time of the 1922 Washington Naval Conference, which set warship tonnage ratios for the United States, Britain and Japan, the Black Chamber was reading Japanese diplomatic messages easily.

Then the Navy started its own codebreaking operation after agents of the Office of Naval Intelligence, the Federal Bureau of Investigation and the New York Police Department broke into the Japanese Consulate in New York, photographed copies of Japanese Navy codebooks and replaced the originals. The Navy hired a former Quaker missionary to Japan, Dr. Emerson J. Haaworth, to translate the books. It was a three-year job, during which Haaworth kept his translation in a red binder: thus the translations became known as the Red Code.

Realizing that the Japanese might change their code at any moment, the Navy decided to expand its codebreaking effort. So a program was started to teach naval officers the Japanese language, a staff of codebreakers was formed and radio intercept stations were set up in Guam and the Philippines to provide the code experts with a flow of Japanese radio traffic. The program was coordinated in 1924 under what was called the Research Desk, in the Office of Naval Communications.

Soon afterward a remarkable codebreaker, Mrs. Agnes Meyer Driscoll, quarreled with her boss in the Army codebreaking service and went to work for the Navy Research Desk. For years she was the Navy's chief authority on Japanese codes and its most talented codebreaker. In 1930 the Japanese suddenly changed their diplomatic and naval codes. Mrs. Driscoll, Thomas H. Dyer, who then was in charge of the Research Desk, and their numerous assistants tackled the job of breaking the new code, which they called Blue. Their efforts were greatly aided by a punch-card system conceived by the International Business Machine Company which was a forerunner of the computer, and Blue Code was broken in 1933.

Meantime another talented Navy codebreaker named Jack S. Holtwick broke a new code used by Japanese naval attachés which was not as complicated as Blue Code. Holtwick developed a fantastic device he called the Red Machine, which helped decode Japanese messages. By spying on the Japanese with the Red Machine the Navy learned all kinds of astonishing things. For example, the codebreakers discovered that the Japanese had an accurate radio direction finding system in the Pacific which tracked and pinpointed the locations of American warships. So the Navy developed a direction finding system of its own which tracked Japanese vessels from stations in the Philippines, Samoa and Dutch Harbor, Alaska.

After 1937 the work of the codebreakers became increasingly difficult as the Japanese moved into more complex code systems. In codebreaking possibly more than in any other effort the Navy and Army showed a fine spirit of cooperation. Both services agreed that the highest priority should go to breaking the new Japanese diplomatic code called Purple. This task was taken over by the Army under the direction of William Friedman while the Navy processed the other systems. For nineteen months of 1939 and 1940 the Purple Code defied the Army experts. But then an Army codebreaker named Harry L. Clark developed a small, hand-built machine which was a maze of rotors, wiring and switches geared to a keyboard. By means of this device Purple Code was broken.

Meanwhile, at Navy, Mrs. Driscoll, Dyer and Wesley A. Wright worked on a new Japanese code which they called Black. By 1940 they could read Black Code with about 50 to 60 percent efficiency. When Dyer was transferred to Pearl Harbor he took along some coding material which he stored in a safe. In spare time he kept working at Black in an effort to improve the reading of that code. Gradually he created a codebreaking unit at Pearl which was called Hypo, for "Hawaii"—"hypo" being the prewar Navy phonetic designation for the letter *H*. A similar unit was formed at the Cavite Naval Base outside Manila and was called Cast, for "Cavite" in phonetic designation. The third Navy codebreaking operation in Washington was called Negat, for "Navy Department." The descriptive term for the work performed was signal intelligence.

Hypo received a new chief, Lieutenant Commander Joseph J.

Rochefort, in mid-1941. A former enlisted man and not a Naval Academy graduate, Rochefort was one of the most brilliant of the Navy codebreakers. The staff working under him was unsurpassed for talent.

At Cast the chief was Lieutenant Rudolph J. Fabian, who in September 1941 was ordered to transfer his unit's operations from Cavite to a tunnel on Corregidor.

In the flurry of messages and changing codes during the increasingly tense fall days of 1941, a warning finger was pointed at Pearl Harbor. On October 9 and 10 and again on November 15 and 18, Japanese agents in Honolulu were ordered to make precise reports on the locations of warships in Pearl Harbor. For some reason none of these ever reached Admiral Kimmel.

The message that fascinated American intelligence officers most was one Tokyo sent all Japanese embassies on November 19. It was decoded and translated as follows:

REGARDING THE BROADCAST OF A SPECIAL MESSAGE IN EMERGENCY. IN CASE OF EMERGENCY (CUTTING OFF OF DIPLOMATIC RELATIONS) AND THE CUTTING OFF OF INTERNATIONAL COMMUNICATIONS, THE FOLLOWING WARNING WILL BE ADDED IN THE MIDDLE OF THE DAILY JAPANESE LANGUAGE SHORTWAVE NEWS BROADCAST:

1. IN CASE OF JAPAN-U.S. RELATIONS IN DANGER: "EAST WIND, RAIN."

2. IN CASE OF JAPAN-USSR RELATIONS IN DANGER: "NORTH WIND, CLOUDY."

3. IN CASE OF JAPAN-BRITISH RELATIONS IN DANGER: "WEST WIND, CLEAR."

THIS SIGNAL WILL BE GIVEN IN THE MIDDLE AND AT THE END AS A WEATHER FORECAST AND EACH SENTENCE WILL BE REPEATED TWICE. WHEN THIS IS HEARD PLEASE DESTROY ALL CODE PAPERS, ETC. THIS IS AS YET TO BE A COMPLETELY SECRET ARRANGEMENT. FORWARD AS URGENT INTELLIGENCE.

A 24-hour watch on Japanese news broadcasts was immediately set up at Hypo, Cast and Negat. A junior language officer newly arrived at Cast from Tokyo, Thomas R. Mackie, was translating a long, dull economic report from Radio Tokyo when he came upon the Morse code signal "TOOFUUUU" set off by double parentheses.

Chinese and Japanese characters are sent in Morse code by using complex combinations of letters. "TOOFUUUU" represented Chinese characters which, translated, meant "East wind, rain." Believing this was warning that Japanese-American relations were in danger, Mackie rushed the report to his superiors. To his distress they did not believe it significant. They maintained that such an important message definitely would be broadcast in Japanese, not Chinese.

Blair writes in *Silent Victory:*

> Mackie was furious and brooded over the lapse for years. He believed that had an alert been sent, Washington might have more forcefully warned Admiral Kimmel of danger, thus preventing the Pearl Harbor attack.

The entire signal intelligence program in the Pacific was extremely complex, as Potter points out in *Nimitz.* The operations at Hypo under Rochefort, for example, included analyzing enemy traffic, locating and tracking enemy transmitters and using cryptanalysis to decode the messages.

By early 1942 the number of receiving stations with high-frequency direction-finders had been greatly expanded. These stations, listening continually to Japanese transmissions and pinpointing their transmitters, poured their information into Hypo, Cast and Negat. Their traffic analysts could—in theory, at least—forecast the direction and weight of enemy movements by studying the volume and destination of messages. Japanese transmitters, both on ships and at shore bases, tried to conceal their identities by changing their number-letter call signs often. But sensitive analysts quickly identified them again by recognizing the operator's touch on the key—his "fist," as they called it—which was as distinctive as a human voice.

Hypo specialized in the Japanese Navy's operational code, which the Americans called JN25. This code consisted of about 45,000 five-digit groups—figures such as 63975, 87451 and the like—which represented words or phrases. In order to confuse American cryptanalysts the Japanese issued a book of 50,000 random five-digit groups to their communicators. When messages were sent, a series of these random groups was added to the message code groups. In the message a key five-digit group told a receiver the page, column and line in the random-group book where the sender had chosen his first group. The receiver located the same place in his own random-group book. After weeding out the meaningless random numbers, he looked up the remaining groups in the decode book to learn what the message said. As further frustrations to cryptanalysts the Japanese occasionally issued new random-group books or scrambled their code groups.

The Navy, and especially the station at Hypo, had extraordinarily skilled cryptanalysts who were aided by the heavy traffic in Japanese Navy code. With traffic often running as high as 1,000 messages a day, the same random groups and code groups inevitably came together again and again. This enabled the Americans to use a mathematical process to discover the basic code groups. These then were cracked by standard cryptographic methods.

Potter writes:

Only a fraction of the 45,000 meanings that the JN code groups represented was ever brought to light by cryptanalysis. The codebreakers, after weeks of attacking a new version of the code, were lucky to recover 15 percent of any message text. This much, however, when combined with the results of traffic analysis and related to previously recorded message fragments, was usually enough to yield useful information. The IBM tabulators, which stored on cards quantities of data from the radio dispatches, did most of the work of connecting new messages with old ones. Equally important in this process was the fantastic memory of Commander Rochefort, who could recall details of enemy messages filed weeks earlier.*

Employing such codebreaking methods, the Cast unit put together early in April intelligence that Rochefort at Hypo called a "fantastic piece of work."

The 75 men of Cast were evacuated from Corregidor in mid-March after Manila fell by the submarines *Permit* and *Seadragon*. With their precious equipment they rendezvoused in Melbourne, Australia, still under the command of Fabian, and within a couple of days they were once more an operational organization exchanging information with Hypo at Pearl Harbor and Negat in Washington.

Soon after Cast arrived in Melbourne it assembled intelligence indicating that the Japanese planned a two-pronged attack in the Southwest Pacific. One target would be Tulagi in the Solomon Islands. The other would be Port Moresby, a strategic location on the southeast coast of New Guinea only 270 miles from Australia. As usual in signal intelligence, the Cast codebreakers obtained only bits and pieces of tactical information from which they and their superiors had to divine strategic intentions. They predicted that the Port Moresby invasion force would be convoyed by Japanese Carrier Division 5: two heavy carriers besides a light carrier and many cruisers and destroyers.

Cast's conclusion set the stage for what would become the first engagement of aircraft carriers in history. It would be known as the Battle of the Coral Sea.

---

* *Nimitz.*

7

Battle of the Coral Sea

A boxer pressing for a knockout may overreach and find himself in trouble. Something like that was happening to the Japanese in the spring of 1942. They had come so far in such a brief time that they seemed to feel there was no limit to their luck.

Yamamoto's grand strategy was not at first totally apparent to the Americans. It was revealed bit by bit through the diligence and skill of the codebreakers. The first revelation came from Cast with the report of the planned attack against Tulagi and Port Moresby.

Actually it was quite an elaborate plan, for Japanese strategists liked to divide their forces. It called for three chief divisions of naval strength. A left prong under Rear Admiral Kiyohide Shima would occupy Tulagi, in the lower Solomons, where it would establish an air base. At the same time a right prong of transports escorted by heavy cruisers and the light carrier *Shoho* under Rear Admiral Kajioka would start from Rabaul, on New Britain, and come down around the eastern tip of New Guinea to take Port Moresby. Covering these groups and ready to destroy any Allied resistance to the plan was a big striking force under Vice Admiral Takeo Takagi which included the large carriers *Shokaku* and *Zuikaku,* veterans of the Pearl Harbor attack. The entire operation was under the direction of Vice Admiral Shigeyoshi Inouye in Rabaul. And watching everything closely from Tokyo was Yamamoto, who kept in steady radio communication.

After the codebreakers alerted Nimitz to Japanese intentions in the Southwest Pacific, he wished for Halsey. But that fighting admiral, along with Spruance and the carriers *Enterprise* and *Hornet,* was involved in the Tokyo raid. What Spruance feared had come to pass: Task Force 16 was engaged in an operation good for nothing but Stateside morale when it was urgently needed in the Coral Sea.

Nimitz patched together what forces he could to try to check the enemy in the southwest. He ordered Rear Admiral Aubrey W. Fitch in the carrier *Lexington* to hasten from Pearl Harbor and rendezvous in the Coral Sea with the carrier *Yorktown,* commanded by Fletcher, who was the senior officer but had less carrier experience than Fitch. The carriers were to be joined by two Australian cruisers—*Australia* and *Hobart*—and the American cruiser *Chicago* plus a few destroyers, all under the command of Rear Admiral J. G. Crace of the Royal Navy.

Nimitz was summoned to San Francisco for a conference with King. There the two pondered, among many things, if Fletcher was sufficiently in control of his carrier task force all the time and if he was aggressive enough for successful operations against the enemy. Nimitz believed in giving subordinates every possible chance to succeed—and Fletcher had not yet really been put to the test in combat. But King harbored prejudices. Whatever questions the two had about Fletcher's aggressive leadership, there was nothing they could do at that point. Halsey and Spruance would return to Pearl April 25 from the Tokyo raid. Halsey would need five days to resupply his force and then was to sail for the Coral Sea on April 30.

Nimitz very much wanted Halsey to be in command of the operations there, but would events await his arrival with Spruance and the task force? Having learned to anticipate the worst in this Pacific war, Nimitz hoped that if Halsey did not arrive in time Fletcher and Fitch with *Yorktown* and *Lexington* could thwart the Japanese with the aid of land-based aircraft from Australia and Samoa.

The Coral Sea is one of the loveliest areas of the Pacific Ocean. Morison is lyrical about it in *The Two-Ocean War:*

> Typhoons pass it by; the southeast trades blow fresh across its surface almost the entire year, raising whitecaps which build up to long surges that crash on Australia's Great Barrier Reef in a 1500-mile line of white foam. Lying between the Equator and the Tropic of Capricorn, it knows no winter, and the summer is never uncomfortably hot. The islands on the eastern and northern verges—New Caledonia, the New Hebrides, the Louisiades—are lofty, jungle-clad and ringed with coral beaches and reefs. Here the interplay of bright sunlight, pure air and transparent water may be seen at its best; peacock-hued shoals over the coral gardens break off abruptly from an emerald-hued fringe into deeps of brilliant amethyst. . . .

But the events unfolding in the Coral Sea in the spring of 1942 were anything but beautiful. They were tragic, as only death can be. They were confused, as only war can be. If the opposing forces had been playing games instead of shooting for blood, the high rate of human error involved might have seemed funny.

On May 3 Shima's force occupied Tulagi without opposition. Next day Fletcher came close with *Yorktown*, whose planes bombed Tulagi without much damage. The Japanese defenders called for help. It was a perfect situation for the carriers *Shokaku* and *Zuikaku* to team up against *Yorktown*. But they were far off at Rabaul, delivering nine airplanes to save an extra ferrying mission. This example of petty thrift cost the Japanese a great opportunity.

For the next two days the opposing forces groped around seeking one another. Once they were only seventy miles apart. Both sides were hampered by a wide strip of clouds and showers stretching across the Coral Sea. The radar equipment of the time was short-range and not very effective. Both sides depended on visual spotting by planes.

On the morning of May 7 the two big Japanese flattops sent out scout planes which reported sighting a carrier and a cruiser. What the scouts actually sighted were the American fleet oiler *Neosho* and destroyer *Sims,* which had withdrawn from the main body of the task force to complete a refueling operation. Takagi ordered a full force bombing mission against the American vessels. *Sims* accounted for six enemy planes before she was sunk along with *Neosho*. This diversion saved the American carriers from attack, but the loss of a fleet tanker was especially wounding.

At the time Takagi's planes were attacking their misidentified targets Americans were also making mistakes. When a scout plane reported two Japanese carriers and four heavy cruisers about 175 miles northwest of the American carriers, Fletcher naturally presumed the scout plane had located Takagi's main force. What the American pilot actually had seen was two heavy cruisers and two destroyers. And what the attackers from *Lexington* and *Yorktown* found when they sped to the area was the Japanese light carrier *Shoho*. The American bombers sank her in ten minutes—a record short time for sinking a carrier throughout the war. The sinking disturbed Inouye in Rabaul, and he ordered the Port Moresby invasion force to pause and await for further developments.

Of course Fletcher didn't know that the invasion force had turned back temporarily. He sent Crace with his three cruisers and a few destroyers to intercept it. What Crace and his ships came upon, instead of the invaders, was a flight of 31 enemy land-based bombers from Rabaul which dived on them like a swarm of angry bees. The Allied vessels handled themselves so well that they were not damaged seriously. The surviving Japanese attackers flew back to Rabaul, where they reported they had sunk two battleships and a heavy cruiser.

Crace's men were congratulating themselves on having fought off the Japanese strike without damage when they were attacked again. This time the attackers were three U. S. Army B-17s from Australia who mistook the Allied cruisers and destroyers for the main Japanese fleet. It was a stand-off with no damage among friends except for some intense embarrassment later in the U. S. Army Air Force, where it appeared that crews were not studying their enemy identification charts hard enough.

Frustration was making Takagi frantic. Toward evening he sent out a big search-attack mission to find and bomb the American carriers. The Japanese planes couldn't find the carriers, but they were found themselves by American fighters which shot down nine of them. As darkness fell the Japanese fliers were thoroughly confused. Six tried to land on *Yorktown,* mistaking her for Japanese, and eleven more were lost when they tried to land on their own flattops after dark.

Shortly after dawn of the next day, May 8, planes of each side discovered their enemy's carriers, and soon the battle was joined. Fletcher had decided on May 5 to make the carrier-wise Fitch the officer in tactical command in battle, but through some foul-up of communications Fitch did not hear about it till 0830 on May 8 as Fletcher was preparing to launch *Yorktown's* planes.

The sides were evenly matched. The Japanese had 121 planes, the Americans 122. In the screening forces the Americans had one more heavy cruiser and one more destroyer than the enemy. But luck favored the Japanese in one important respect: Their carriers were cloaked by the band of clouds and fog that stretched across the area. The Americans, on the other hand, were out in bright sunlight where they afforded the enemy easily visible targets.

Yorktown attackers could not find *Zuikaku,* which was hidden by a rain squall; they concentrated on *Shokaku* and hit her with three bombs. One of these bent the flight deck so that she could not launch more planes until sent home for repairs. *Lexington* planes also failed to find *Zuikaku* and managed to hit *Shokaku* only once. The American torpedo attacks were ineffective, with torpedoes failing to explode on apparent contacts. Pilots had been insisting for some time that there was something seriously wrong with American warheads—and submariners were making the same complaint about their torpedoes.

Meanwhile the Japanese were severely mauling the American carriers. *Yorktown* took an 800-pound bomb which penetrated four decks and killed or wounded 66 men. Four bombs hit *Lexington,* and then she suffered strikes by two torpedoes shot into her by bombers flying a few feet above the waves. "Lady Lex," as sailors called her, began to list, and three fires burning below decks sent black clouds of smoke into the blue sky. Her power plant was still operating, and Captain Frederick Sherman believed his men could put out the flames and get the big flattop away to safety. But then *Lexington* shuddered suddenly to the thunder of an internal explosion. Pockets of gas fumes had collected from ruptured gasoline lines and a single spark from a generator had been enough to set off the explosion. Another followed —and then another, until it was apparent *Lexington* could not be saved. After Sherman ordered Abandon Ship it was carried out in perfect order. About 150 wounded were lowered over the side in basket stretchers and placed in lifeboats while others went down lines into the water, where destroyers picked up survivors quickly.

By noon the battle was ended. Takagi, thinking both American carriers were sinking, felt free to send *Shokaku* back to Japan for repairs. *Yorktown* was hurt all right, but not mortally. Once the internal explosions began to rack *Lexington,* she was finished. A friendly torpedo sent her to the bottom of the Coral Sea.

The bodies of 216 men and remains of 36 planes sank with her. A total of 2,735 men were rescued and 19 planes taken aboard *Yorktown.* For reasons that usually have to do with the quality of their officers, some ships inspire affection from their crews as if they were human beings. *Lexington* was one of these.

A surviving crewman of *Lexington,* Jack Smith, said later, "I couldn't watch her go, and men who had been with her since she was commissioned in '27 stood with tears streaming."*

Inouye, weighing the loss of *Shoho* and the departure of *Shokaku* for repairs, decided to call off the Port Moresby invasion. He reasoned that land-based American bombers which ranged the New Guinea coasts made it too great a risk, now that Japanese air power had been so depleted by the sea battles.

Yamamoto, watching all from Tokyo, where a stream of messages kept him thoroughly informed, was angry that Inouye gave up so easily. Uncertain about the report that both American carriers had been sunk, Yamamoto ordered Takagi to have *Zuikaku* seek out and sink both carriers if they were still afloat. *Zuikaku* started the hunt just before darkness fell, but by that time it was too late: The Japanese could not find *Yorktown.*

Still the comedy of errors continued. On the morning of May 9 a *Yorktown* search plane reported a Japanese carrier 175 miles distant. Dive bombers roared off the deck while the Army Air Force, alerted at once, sent 14 B-17s from an Australian base. It was perhaps the most perfectly coordinated attack by Army and Navy planes to that point in the war. There was only one difficulty: The enemy flattop turned out to be one of the many small, flat, deserted islands in the Coral Sea.

Both sides publicly claimed victory. Privately both Nimitz and Yamamoto may have ground their teeth a bit. The Americans had lost a carrier, a destroyer and a tanker sunk and a carrier wounded, which left them only two carriers—*Hornet* and *Enterprise*—ready for immediate battle duty in the Central and Southwest Pacific. The

* Morison, *History of U.S. Naval Operations in World War II: Coral Sea, Midway and Submarine Actions,* Vol. 4, (Boston: Little, Brown, 1949).

Japanese had lost a light carrier sunk and a heavy carrier temporarily put away for repairs. While the Japanese called off their Port Moresby invasion, they still held Tulagi.

Morison, in retrospect, is more positive about the American accomplishment in the Battle of the Coral Sea than were some commanders at the time. He points out that besides *Shokaku* being laid up for repairs, *Zuikaku* lost so many planes that she did not return to duty until June. Thus both of these big carriers were unable to serve in the crucial battle that now was imminent: the Battle of Midway.

海軍省許可濟第七八○號

"Battleship Row" in flames during the Japanese attack on Pearl Harbor December 7, 1941. This view from an aerial attacker was captured from the Japanese.

The magazine of Destroyer *Shaw* explodes in the attack by Japanese planes at Pearl Harbor.

A fireboat fights the flames aboard Battleship *West Virginia* at Pearl Harbor.

Battleship *California* reels from a hit by an enemy bomb.

Smoke and flames engulf Battleships *West Virginia* and *Tennessee* while Japanese bombs fall on Pearl Harbor.

Fleet Admiral Chester W. Nimitz.

Admiral Raymond A. Spruance.

Vice Admiral Frank Jack Fletcher.

Admirals Spruance and Nimitz on shipboard later in the war.

Carrier *Enterprise* under way in the Pacific. In the background is Carrier *Lexington*.

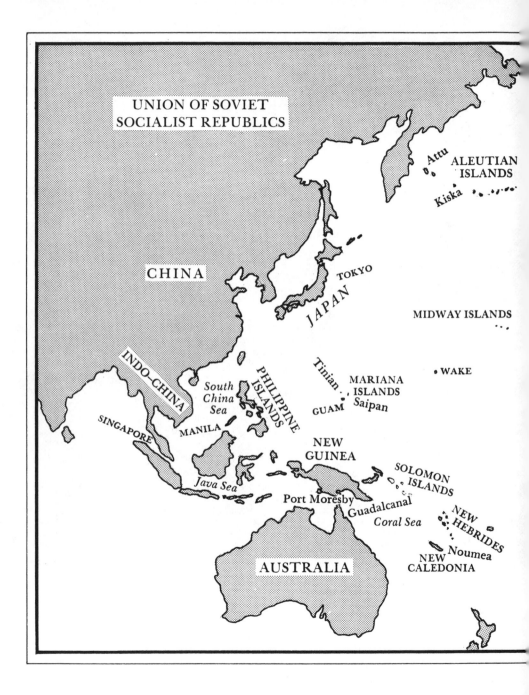

UNION OF SOVIET
SOCIALIST REPUBLICS

ALEUTIAN
ISLANDS

Attu

Kiska

CHINA

JAPAN

TOKYO

MIDWAY ISLANDS

INDO-CHINA

WAKE

South
China
Sea

PHILIPPINE ISLANDS

Tinian

MARIANA
ISLANDS

SINGAPORE

MANILA

GUAM

Saipan

NEW
GUINEA

SOLOMON
ISLANDS

Java Sea

Port Moresby

Guadalcanal

Coral Sea

NEW
HEBRIDES

Noumea

NEW
CALEDONIA

AUSTRALIA

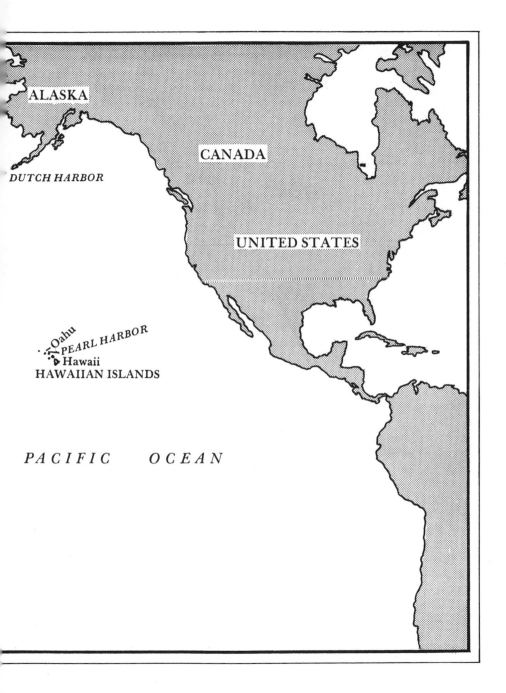

ALASKA

CANADA

DUTCH HARBOR

UNITED STATES

Oahu
PEARL HARBOR
Hawaii
HAWAIIAN ISLANDS

PACIFIC   OCEAN

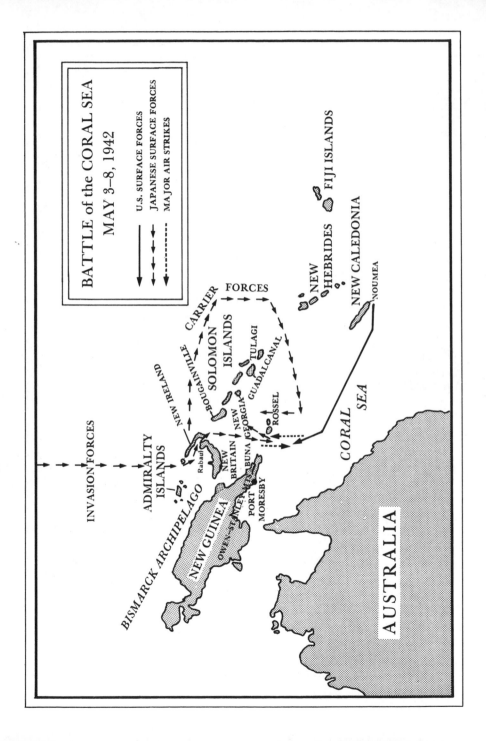

BATTLE of the CORAL SEA
MAY 3–8, 1942

U.S. SURFACE FORCES
JAPANESE SURFACE FORCES
MAJOR AIR STRIKES

INVASION FORCES

ADMIRALTY ISLANDS

BISMARCK ARCHIPELAGO

NEW GUINEA

OWEN-STANLEY

PORT MORESBY

Rabaul

NEW BRITAIN

BUNA

NEW IRELAND

BOUGAINVILLE

SOLOMON ISLANDS

CARRIER FORCES

NEW GEORGIA

TULAGI

GUADALCANAL

ROSSEL

CORAL SEA

NEW HEBRIDES

FIJI ISLANDS

NEW CALEDONIA

NOUMEA

AUSTRALIA

Crewmen abandon the burning Carrier *Lexington* after she is hit in the
Battle of the Coral Sea. Destroyers stand by for rescue work.

All hands have abandoned Carrier *Lexington* as fires rage on her flight deck and superstructure. Soon after this photo was taken a friendly torpedo sent her to the bottom of the sea. "I couldn't watch her go," a crewman said. "Men who had been with her since she was commissioned stood with tears streaming."

Japanese Carrier *Akagi,* veteran of the attack on Pearl Harbor, which came to grief under American bombing at the Battle of Midway.

Japanese Heavy Cruiser *Mikuma* afire and sinking after being raked by American bombers in the Battle of Midway.

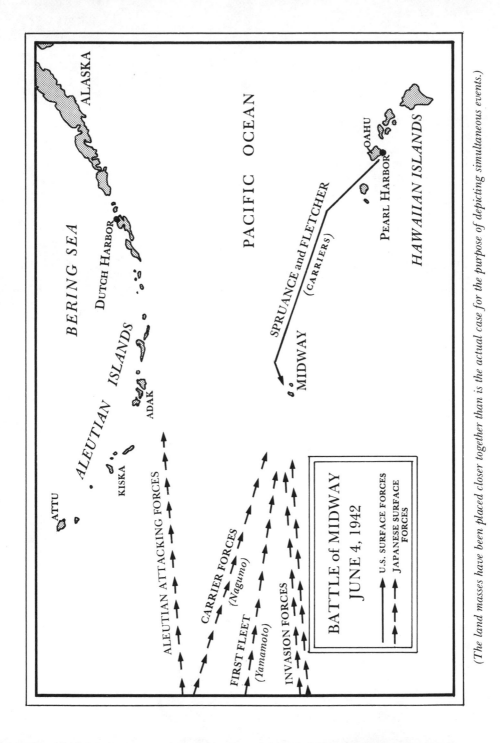

ALASKA

ALEUTIAN ISLANDS

ATTU

KISKA

ADAK

DUTCH HARBOR

BERING SEA

PACIFIC OCEAN

OAHU

PEARL HARBOR

HAWAIIAN ISLANDS

SPRUANCE and FLETCHER
(CARRIERs)

MIDWAY

ALEUTIAN ATTACKING FORCES

CARRIER FORCES
(*Naguumo*)

FIRST FLEET
(*Yamamoto*)

INVASION FORCES

BATTLE of MIDWAY
JUNE 4, 1942

→ U.S. SURFACE FORCES

⇒ JAPANESE SURFACE
FORCES

(The land masses have been placed closer together than is the actual case for the purpose of depicting simultaneous events.)

Crewmen on the flight deck of Carrier *Yorktown* keep cool after
enemy bombs have damaged her in the Battle of Midway. They
believe they can save her.

Antiaircraft guns from *Yorktown* and the warships screening her still throw up protective fire against Japanese planes after the first hit.

Further enemy attacks damage *Yorktown* critically and she begins to list heavily. Her crew of about 2,000 abandons ship. But the Navy still hopes to save *Yorktown*. A salvage crew is put aboard her. Destroyer *Hammann* (right) comes along side to provide her with auxiliary power.

Stealthily the Japanese Submarine *I-168* has crept in through the American destroyer screen and quickly fired four torpedoes. One misses, two pass beneath *Hammann* and deal fatal blows to *Yorktown*. The fourth hits *Hammann*; this shows *Yorktown* going down in four minutes with great loss of life. *(All photographs are official U. S. Navy)*

8

Where Is AF?

Soon after Chester Nimitz became CINCPAC at Pearl Harbor he was taken on a tour of the Hypo codebreaking installation in the windowless, closely guarded basement of the 14th Naval District administration building. He had a low opinion of Rochefort's operation. If there really was anything solid about this traffic analysis and decoding of enemy messages, Nimitz thought, why hadn't Hypo been able to forecast the attack on Pearl?

Before long, however, Nimitz was impressed by Lieutenant Commander Edwin T. Layton, who had been Kimmel's intelligence officer and whom Nimitz retained in the same capacity. Layton expected that his would be one of the first heads to roll because he had not been able to warn Kimmel of the attack. But Nimitz was struck by the younger man's understanding of Japanese psychology and his detailed knowledge of the enemy fleet. Indeed, Layton became the only officer besides Nimitz himself who was permanently assigned to the CINCPAC staff throughout the war. Gradually Layton explained that much of what he knew came from the work of his friend Joe Rochefort and the Navy's codebreaking operation. He made Nimitz realize that the codebreakers' failure to give warning of the Pearl

Harbor attack was a result of Japanese code changes which the American experts had not been able to crack before the fateful Sunday. Thus the new CINCPAC came to depend heavily on the signal intelligence the codebreakers supplied him through Layton.

The warning from Cast of the Port Moresby-Tulagi invasions made Nimitz regret that Halsey with two aircraft carriers was off bombing Tokyo—an operation he never had favored, though he had found it necessary to bow to the will of King in the matter. As soon as Halsey and Spruance returned from the Tokyo raid, Nimitz of course sent them on toward the Coral Sea as quickly as possible. He doubted they would arrive in time with *Enterprise* and *Hornet*—and his doubts proved well founded.

Headquarters at Pearl Harbor learned of developments in the Coral Sea battle spottily and in fragments. Much of the early information came from Army Air Force sources, since the naval force kept radio silence as long as feasible. Some of the information was false; early hopes at headquarters of a great American victory were soon dashed. Since even those on the scene of battle were vague about much that was happening, the picture was even more confusing at a distance. It was a period of tense waiting at Pearl Harbor; Nimitz took out his frustration by banging away on the pistol range more than usual.

As soon as the results of the Coral Sea engagement became clear, Nimitz ordered Halsey to turn his task force around and bring it back to Pearl. He also ordered Fletcher to bring in damaged *Yorktown* as fast as possible. For new events were unfolding—events of which Nimitz gave the returning admirals some inkling through coded messages.

Rochefort had drawn up a four-part estimate of enemy intentions on the basis of his intelligence sources: (1) The Japanese had penetrated far into the Indian Ocean, but now they were turning back and did not intend to advance farther west. (2) They did not plan to invade Australia. (3) They wanted to establish a base in southeast New Guinea at Port Moresby. (4) Their movement in New Guinea would be followed by a massive action, probably involving the Japanese Combined Fleet, in the Central Pacific.

The first three estimates by Rochefort had been demonstrated to be true. What would be the targets of the Japanese in the Central Pacific?

Immediately after the Battle of the Coral Sea, Imperial Naval Headquarters in Tokyo began sending a huge flow of messages preparing the fleet for action. As usual, the codebreakers agonized over the gaps they could not read in enemy messages. One thing they did establish, however: the code designation of the enemy's primary objective was "AF." But where was AF?

Admiral King back in Washington thought it meant Hawaii. The Army thought it was the west coast of the United States. Some on the CINCPAC staff believed it was the Aleutians. Rochefort himself, with his amazing intuition, was certain it was Midway, 1,135 miles west-northwest of Pearl Harbor. Nimitz was inclined to think it was either Midway or Hawaii, or both.

Rochefort settled the argument with a clever subterfuge. Away back in 1903 the Pacific Commercial Cable Company had established a station at Midway on its underwater cable connection between Honolulu, Guam and Manila. Over this closed-circuit cable Rochefort and Layton ordered the naval station at Midway to send out a plain-language radio message announcing that the fresh water evaporators had broken down and the water supply was limited. Before long Hypo's counterpart in Japan, the Owada Communications Group, sent a message to Admiral Yamamoto saying AF was short of fresh water.

The entire atoll called Midway was only six miles in diameter. It enclosed two little islets—Sand and Eastern—and a fair harbor. Sand Island was less than two miles long and Eastern a little more than one; both islets were protected by a barrier reef a few feet above sea level. This bit of real estate, which a Yankee skipper claimed for his country in 1859, had long been considered of little worth. But that changed after the airplane became a weapon of war. Strategically, in the words of Admiral Nagumo, "Midway Island acts as a sentry for Hawaii."

Originally it was one of the more desolate spots on earth. It was not blessed with lovely Polynesian girls, coconut palms or anything else of beauty. Sand, rough coral, wind, hot sun, gooney birds and stinging flies were the elements that combined to drive men mad, as they used to say, in the long ago when a detachment of twenty marines was kept there to guard the cable station, a forlorn lighthouse, and—in the days of steam—a coaling station.

Gradually those who went to Midway began to give the atoll a new look, however. Sand Island was developed into a pleasant garden spot of shrubs, lawns, ironwood and eucalyptus trees. In 1935 Pan American Airways made Sand Island a stop for its trans-Pacific Clippers. A small hotel and tennis courts were built. The Navy soon afterward designated Midway an air station. By the summer of 1941 Sand Island had a town of hundreds of inhabitants—construction workers, a Marine defense battalion and others—with fuel tanks, a large seaplane hangar and many buildings. Meantime a 5,300-foot runway for land-based planes was completed on Eastern Island across the ship channel from Sand.

Two Japanese destroyers had bombarded Midway on the night of December 7 in conjunction with the Pearl Harbor raid but did little damage. In the following days the garrison was reinforced with men and planes. Midway assumed an importance such as no one had imagined a half-century previously. For, after the Japanese took Wake, Midway became the westernmost American base in the Pacific. One of its advantages was that it was beyond the range of Wake-based Japanese planes, so the enemy did not know what was happening there.

Nimitz, drawing most of his evidence from Hypo intelligence, finally concluded that Midway was indeed the primary target of the next Japanese move.

Pressures on Nimitz grew after the Battle of the Coral Sea, but he did not flinch under them. The American situation in the Pacific was truly desperate in May 1942. Japan had ten aircraft carriers, while the Americans had available only two—maybe three, if *Yorktown* could be made serviceable quickly.

For all Nimitz really knew at first, Yamamoto planned another attack on Pearl Harbor. The operable battleships there had become a liability rather than an asset in the new age of air power, so Nimitz sent them to safety on the mainland west coast. Some of the older "battleship admirals," who still could not bring themselves to believe in the strength of the airplane, criticized him for this, but Nimitz had sent them to the mainland because they were too slow to accompany the carriers.

Nimitz was also pressured by the British, who had not yet become the helpful allies in the Pacific they sincerely wished to be. After surrendering Singapore and giving up Burma without a fight, the British were in defeatist mood. When a powerful Japanese naval force steamed into the Indian Ocean in April, Britain scratched together a naval force of five obsolete battleships and three small carriers under Admiral Sir John Somerville that was no match against their strong enemy. While the Japanese attacked Ceylon (now Sri Lanka) and sank two cruisers and a carrier, Somerville took the rest of his force into hiding at remote Addu Atoll, 600 miles southwest of Ceylon. The Japanese, clearly having no intention of advancing farther because they were already overextended, fell back and never returned to the Indian Ocean. But some of the British, obsessed by the notion the Japanese intended to invade Madagascar and link up with the Germans in the Middle East, begged for American naval support that Nimitz did not have and certainly would not have sent on pointless adventures in distant seas.

At that time the U.S. Army was proving more troublesome to Nimitz's and King's ideas of how to prosecute the war than were the British allies.

MacArthur believed the Japanese were about to renew their offensive in New Guinea and the Solomons. He was urging increased naval support for his area even while Nimitz was gathering his weak remaining forces to deal with Yamamoto's main thrust at Midway.

But to CINCPAC's mind the Army Air Force was acting even more difficult than Douglas MacArthur. For some reason the Army had become obsessed with the notion the Japanese were going to make an air attack on San Francisco. So it would not release from the mainland all the bombers Nimitz felt he would need at Midway. In response he ordered nearly all available Army bombers in Hawaii forward to the advanced base. Major General Delos C. Emmons, who had succeeded the fired General Short as Army commander in Hawaii, was grievously upset at having his bombers taken from him.

Every day brought mounting evidence from Hypo intelligence that the Japanese intended to seize Midway. Nearly every day, too, came fresh bad news of some sort. For example, Admiral Fitch radioed from *Yorktown* that it would take ninety days to restore the carrier to full operational capability.

In early May Nimitz decide to go to Midway and find out for himself what the situation was. Flying there, he spent an entire day crawling around gun pits and underground command posts while questioning the defenders and inspecting their arms. Pleased by their preparedness and the cooperative spirit between Commander Cyril T. Simard, the Midway naval commander, and Marine Lieutenant Colonel Harold Shannon, in charge of ground forces, Nimitz asked what they needed to defend the atoll against a major amphibious assault. They provided a list, to which the Commander in Chief added.

Returning to Pearl Harbor, Nimitz sent Midway the converted railroad ferry *Kittyhawk* laden with 18 dive-bombers, 7 Wildcat fighters, 5 light tanks, a number of antiaircraft guns and the men necessary to serve these new weapons. A few days later he sent two Marine rifle companies and a 37-millimeter anti-aircraft battery. CINCPAC had to scrounge, for everything was in short supply. The number of Catalina seaplanes and amphibians was increased to 30. The total number of B-17s and B-26s wrenched from Emmons rose to 22. Most of the pilots were fresh out of flight school and had no combat experience; there was such a shortage of ground crews that flight crews had to do most of their own fueling and servicing. Food, medicine, clothing for all these people had to be rushed in. The marines sent more fighter planes with green crews. Then there was a clamor for oilers, tenders, torpedo boats. In scraping around to aid the defenders, the Navy found four converted tuna fishing boats and sent them. Pleas for more and more aviation gasoline came in to Pearl Harbor daily over the closed-circuit cable. When a final load of drummed aviation gas arrived at Midway aboard a chartered freighter on Sunday, May 31, the merchant marine crew suddenly demanded overtime pay to unload it; instead the ship's officers and boatswains manned winches and tended hatches in order that marine enlisted men could unload the precious fuel.

Nimitz was so impressed by the strenuous efforts of Simard and Shannon to secure the defenses of Midway that he had the former promoted to captain and the latter to full colonel. As he remarked to one of his staff in his wry way, "Better to send the flowers before the funeral."

The matter of organizing and supplying the arms and men who would fight in such vital battles as the one coming for Midway was a new technology for the Navy. Until the outbreak of war the armed forces had not given much thought to this military science called logistics—what Napoleon meant when he said, "An army advances on its stomach." The U.S. Army claimed to have learned something about modern logistics by studying the present war in Europe, before America became involved.

The Navy began learning some of its World War II logistics lessons in arming and supplying Midway Atoll. Compared to future big Pacific operations, the task at Midway was minor: the moving, arming and supplying for a few weeks of 121 combat planes, 141 officers and 2,886 enlisted men. But the experiences of Midway would lead to the establishment of a vast, complex organization called Service Force Pacific Fleet, which would perform feats of magic.

Even at the time of Midway, before the Pacific Fleet began to grow, astronomical amounts of fuel were being used. Eventually each attack force would be accompanied by two fleet oilers. Still later there would be roving fueling groups of two or three big oilers convoyed by destroyers. They were like traveling service stations ready to do business at designated spots and refuel combat ships according to a prearranged schedule.

All of this logistic support depended, of course, on a tremendous, coordinated effort at home in the States. Behind Pearl Harbor there began to grow a vast logistic network. It extended through Western Sea Frontier at San Francisco, with its huge warehouse complexes at Oakland and Alameda, to the great collecting depot at Clearfield, Utah. The planners carefully placed this on the eastern slope of the Continental Divide in order to relieve railroad congestion in the Rocky Mountain passes. And behind Clearfield the network extended into every city, town and farm in the United States.

The war, only a few months old, had grown complex and diversified, meaning different things to different people. It was not at all the same for the codebreakers and for those developing a logistics and supply system. To many women it meant leaving home and going to work on assembly lines or at other jobs. To many men it meant leaving their families and traveling to distant places as soldiers or sailors or airmen. But to everyone it meant change, if only to the slight degree of food rationing and minor sacrifices. Americans were joining together in a vast effort as never before in their history. They were releasing reservoirs of industrial strength and skill in torrents of energy. So great were their resources and efforts, indeed, that they became the only people on earth to improve their standard of living at the same time they were prosecuting a world war.

No one knew better than Admiral Yamamoto the threat a united America posed to the imperial ambitions of Japan. He knew he must deal a knockout blow to American power in the Pacific—and quickly. Only with an overwhelming defeat of the U. S. Navy could America be persuaded to quit the struggle in the Pacific and turn its total war efforts to Europe.

Nimitz, with increasing belief in Hypo's signal intelligence, decided on a personal meeting with Rochefort at which the staff skeptics would be present. An hour was set for May 24. The appointed time came and went, but Rochefort did not appear. Nimitz's bright blue eyes took on an icy glint; absolutely no one ever was late for an appointment with him. But Rochefort was late that day: half an hour behind time, acting distraught. Apologizing, he said he and his staff had been up all night trying to break the date-time cipher. One of his assistants, Lieutenant Commander Wesley Wright, finally had succeeded to the extent that Hypo made this prediction: The Japanese would start operations against the Aleutians on June 3 and against Midway on June 4.

The staff skeptics snorted in disbelief. Why would Yamamoto use his entire main fleet to capture a couple of fog-wrapped Aleutian islands and tiny Midway Atoll? They believed the intercepted messages were fakes designed to mislead the Americans to true Japanese intentions. Why would the enemy send such vital top secret information by radio for everyone to read and try to decode?

Maybe, Nimitz replied to the skeptics, because Yamamoto was in such a hurry to carry out his plans that he had to send his orders by radio so everyone would receive them in time. Speaking deliberately, Nimitz raised another thought: Yamamoto's chief purpose might not so much be to acquire small islands and atolls as to draw out the main body of the weak American fleet and destroy it. If he succeeded in that, the Japanese would be close to their goal of turning the western Pacific into a private lake which belonged to the emperor.

Nimitz, in developing his battle plans, weighed enemy capabilities in relation to enemy intentions. In this respect Hypo intelligence was of greater aid to him than any other source. At the same time he assigned an officer the role of devil's advocate: to try to prove Hypo's intelligence wrong in light of a variety of facts, such as the state of Pacific spring weather, winds and currents.

The meticulous Layton slept little, kept consulting Rochefort and brooded like a medieval astrologer in pursuing his assignment. Potter writes in *Nimitz* that the Commander in Chief became impatient with his slowness and urged him to come up with something specific.

"I have a difficult time being specific," Layton said.

"I want you to be specific," Nimitz told him. "After all, this is the job I have given you—to be the admiral commanding the Japanese forces and tell us what you're going to do."

"All right then, Admiral," said Layton. "I've previously given you the intelligence that the carriers will probably attack Midway on the morning of the fourth of June, so we'll pick the fourth of June for the day. They'll come in from the northwest on bearing 325 degrees and they will be sighted at about 175 miles from Midway, and the time will be about 0600 Midway time."

Nowhere is it recorded that Chester Nimitz was left speechless at any time, but just that once he may have paused a moment or two before replying to such specific conclusions by his intelligence officer.

Nimitz began to lay his plans on the assumption that what Layton had told him would be proven true. And he decided that the vital component in the enemy force attacking Midway would be Nagumo's four veteran carriers.

The upperworks of Halsey's task force returning from the southwest came over the horizon at dawn, May 26. After the ships filed into Pearl Harbor, Halsey's barge took him ashore to report to Nimitz.

When the Commander in Chief saw Halsey he was shocked. The fighting admiral had lost twenty pounds, his face was haggard, and his skin had erupted in a painful rash. The nervous strain of having spent nearly six months by day and night on the bridge of *Enterprise* had caused the dermatitis that made restful sleep impossible.

Nimitz had been counting on Halsey to lead the small American force that would challenge the powerful Japanese fleet at Midway. But now that was impossible. Now Halsey, instead of sailing for Midway, would have to go to the hospital.

9

A New Task Force Commander

After Halsey's force came to rest in Pearl Harbor, Admiral Spruance went to pay his customary voyage-end call on his commander aboard *Enterprise*. As his barge reached the platform alongside the carrier, Halsey's flag lieutenant, William H. Ashford, hastened down the accommodation ladder with news.

Halsey had gone to the hospital with acute dermatitis. Admiral Nimitz wanted to see Spruance immediately at headquarters.

Nimitiz was not his usual smiling self when Spruance appeared. A bit grimly he said that the ill Halsey had recommended Spruance command Task Force 16 when it put to sea again and that the recommendation was now an official order.

No doubt Spruance was dismayed, though of course he tried not to show it. Presumably command of a carrier task force required an expert in naval air warfare. Halsey had had eight years of experience in carrier aviation, but Spruance had none.

Nimitz, seeing Spruance's wonder, pointed out that he would have the advantage of working with Halsey's experienced staff aboard *Enterprise*. At first Nimitz had felt stunned by the loss of Halsey, on whom he had counted for tactical leadership in the forthcoming battle. On reflection, however, he found some good in an unhappy situation. Spruance had the capacity to think cooly and act logically under stress, whereas Halsey had an inclination to be impulsively bold. Nimitz liked what he knew about Spruance.

Now, as the two talked about the forthcoming battle, Nimitz was pleased by Spruance's dispassionate view of how it should be fought. He especially liked Spruance's prudent observation that the American carrier force should not go west of Midway in search of the enemy before the Japanese carriers were substantially disabled. Spruance was mindful that if the U.S. force went too far west the enemy might bypass it and attack Pearl Harbor.

Nimitz said Task Force 16 under Spruance had forty-eight hours to refuel and resupply before leaving to take up a position northeast of Midway. *Yorktown* under Fletcher was due to arrive tomorrow; if it could be repaired in time it would join *Enterprise* and *Hornet* under Spruance. Fletcher, being senior to Spruance, would assume tactical command of the American striking force.

As Spruance rose to leave, Nimitz told him casually that after the battle he would come ashore to serve as Nimitz's right-hand man, Chief of Staff of CINCPAC. Nimitz made it sound like a sudden after thought, but actually he had been sizing up Spruance for the job for a long time.

Spruance did not want to be Chief of Staff, as Buell reports in *The Quiet Warrior*. As Spruance said later: "Having had two previous tours of staff duty during my career, I was not too happy about going ashore in the early stages of a big naval war." But he did not show how he felt. He almost never did. And that was one of the main reasons why Nimitz wanted him to be his right-hand man.

Next day *Yorktown*, often called "Waltzing Matilda," hove in view trailing an oil slick ten miles long. Cheers, sirens and whistles greeted her as she entered Pearl Harbor and went straight into drydock. She had barely been secured on blocks and the dock had not been completely drained when Nimitz appeared. Pulling on long rubber boots, he led an inspection party into the depths of the carrier. His inspection was not for show; he knew what he was doing. If the U. S. Navy should ever decide it no longer required the services of Chester Nimitz, he could make a good living as a marine engineer.

Nimitz quickly decided that Fitch's estimate of ninety days to repair the carrier was unrealistic. She had propulsion, her elevators worked and her flight deck already had been repaired on her voyage back from the Coral Sea. Timbers could temporarily brace her bomb-damaged compartments. The most important job was to patch perforations in her hull well enough to keep her going for a couple of weeks longer.

Nimitz, turning to the men in the inspection party, said, "We must have this ship back in three days."

Lieutenant Commander Herbert J. Pfingstad, the hull-repair expert, looked around at everybody in the party. Finally there was no one to look at but Nimitz, who was regarding him icily. "Yes sir," said Pfingstad.

Welding equipment, steel plates and other material began to be assembled within the hour. A total of 1,400 workmen started round-the-clock repairs on *Yorktown*.

After Nimitz returned to his office, Fletcher appeared. They had known each other since undergraduate days at Annapolis. Fletcher looked wilted, not at all like the man who sometimes had been referred to as "Jaunty Jack." Nimitz now faced a distasteful task. Admiral King had taken an increasingly dim view of Fletcher, whom he accused of lacking aggressiveness. King wanted him removed, and Nimitz had to prove to himself that King was right.

Loyalty to loyal friends was as characteristic of Nimitz as the color of his skin—and Fletcher always had been loyal to him. As he began to question his friend intensively about his handling of Task Force 17 in the Coral Sea, it suddenly dawned on Fletcher why he was being questioned thus. Both officers became deeply embarrassed. Fletcher always found it hard to express himself well, and now he became downright tongue-tied. Nimitz, hating his role of carping taskmaster, resorted to an old military dodge. He told his friend Jack to go away and write an explanation of his Task Force 17 command. Fletcher wrote a report which he presented next day. It had the honest ring of truth to Nimitz, who understood how bad luck could cause many a good man to lose ships. He pronounced Fletcher fit for command, and King accepted his pronouncement—for the time being. It may also have crossed Nimitz's mind that with Halsey in the hospital he was running awfully short of carrier admirals.

The codebreakers were supplying CINCPAC with a wonderfully complete picture of Yamamoto's intentions.

The Japanese abandoned plans for a sea invasion of Port Moresby. Instead, they intended to drive overland from Buna, on the north coast of New Guinea. MacArthur naturally was alarmed by this. And so was Nimitz, though for a different reason: It meant all enemy carriers and nearly every warship would be available for Midway.

Rochefort and his staff had more bad news. They estimated that Yamamoto planned to divide his Combined Fleet into three forces: (1) The Northern Force would make a diversionary air raid on the American base at Dutch Harbor in the Aleutians, and then its transports would land troops to occupy the western Aleutian islands of Attu, Kiska and Adak. (2) The First Carrier Striking Force would come down on Midway from the northwest and launch the main attack with an air raid on the atoll. (3) The Midway Invasion Force, coming from Guam and Saipan and approaching Midway from the southwest, would be met at sea and escorted the last 650 miles by the Japanese Second Fleet. A total of 16 Japanese submarines also were committed to the Midway action, 10 to the northeast of the atoll and the others between Midway and Pearl Harbor.

Bad though this news was, Nimitz and his staff found some good in it. They were surprised—and delighted—that Yamamoto was dispersing his forces so widely. By concentrating them he could have knocked off his objectives easily one at a time. For example, he assigned two carriers to the Aleutian attack force. If instead Yamamoto had added those to the four that Rochefort believed were the heart of the First Striking Force, the Japanese would have been invincible at Midway.

Probably Yamamoto thought his forces would take Midway easily anyway. He had no idea of the preparations there; Japanese traffic analysts could not intercept American messages because they were being sent by the closed-circuit underwater cable. Yamamoto may also have been fooled by a ruse of Nimitz, who had a cruiser far down in the Coral Sea sending out floods of phony messages to make it sound like the presence of a task force. Or possibly Yamamoto expected that the initial Japanese attack in the Aleutians would cause Nimitz to send most of his available strength off in that direction and leave Midway naked.

Nimitz, however, organized only a token force of cruisers and destroyers under Rear Admiral Robert A. Theobald to oppose the enemy thrust at the Aleutians. Theobald could not hope to break up a major carrier attack, but he could inflict much damage if he positioned his ships properly. Theobald's nickname was "Fuzzy." He had the reputation of having one of the worst dispositions in the Navy. When Nimitz informed him that the enemy would invade Attu, Kiska and Adak, Theobald thought it nonsense. Why would the Japanese want to take those obscure islands? He saw it as an enemy trick to draw him away from the main attack at Dutch Harbor. So he stationed his force 400 miles south of Kodiak. He might as well have stationed it in San Francisco Bay for all the good it did in that position.

Fortunately Nimitz did not have a Theobald involved at Midway.

Nimitz and Layton briefed Spruance and Fletcher on the basis of the codebreakers' intelligence. The total force defending Midway would be slight compared to that of the attacking enemy. Spruance's Task Force 16 would comprise carriers *Enterprise* and *Hornet* with 6 cruisers and 12 destroyers. Fletcher's Task Force 17 would comprise *Yorktown* with 2 cruisers and 6 destroyers. Fletcher would assume overall command of both forces.

By the codebreakers' calculations they faced overwhelming odds. Rochefort was convinced the First Striking Force would include 4 of the 6 veteran carriers of the Pearl Harbor attack—*Akagi, Kaga, Hiryu* and *Soryu*—with a screen of 2 battleships, 3 cruisers and 11 destroyers. Signal intelligence was even specific about the identities of the ships in the screening force. (Intercepts indicated that *Shokaku* still was undergoing repairs from damage suffered in the Coral Sea and that *Zuikaku* had not been able to replace the pilots she lost in the battle.) The codebreakers were not as specific about the Midway landing force coming from Guam and Saipan, but it was described in general terms and called powerful.

Nimitz's written orders to his admirals were only ten pages long. Wisely, at that stage in the war, he told his subordinates only what should be done, provided all possible means and information for doing it and then left it to the commander on the scene to accomplish the mission. Spruance and Nimitz agreed that a tactical commander should have freedom of action and use his initiative.

A lengthy intelligence supplement to CINCPAC's succinct orders offered a wealth of detail about each of the enemy ships in the force. Few American officers involved in the battle apart from Spruance and Fletcher realized that the invaluable information CINCPAC provided was the result of codebreaking and analysis of enemy traffic. One officer who read the detailed intelligence analysis and did not know its source must have been fond of spy novels, for he remarked that "our man in Tokyo" was worth every cent the Americans must be paying him.

Nimitz ordered Spruance and Fletcher to take up positions northeast of Midway. Thus they would be on the left flank of the force attacking from the northwest. Or, if the codebreakers were wrong and the striking force came from the northeast, they would be in a position to intercept it. The admirals were to inflict maximum damage on the enemy without unnecessarily risking heavy American losses.

The American mission, specifically stated in Nimitz's written orders, was to hold Midway. But in conversation the Commander in Chief told Spruance and Fletcher they were not to hold the atoll at all costs, for it was more important to preserve the invaluable American carriers than to hold Midway. If Midway fell and the American commander preserved his carriers, he knew he would be publicly castigated for losing the atoll. If, however, he saved Midway and lost his carriers he would have disobeyed Nimitz's principle that the carriers were more important. And if he should lose both Midway *and* his carriers, his name probably would go down in infamy as the admiral who lost everything in the most vital battle of the Pacific war.

If the American fleet were to be sunk, Hawaii would be left open to a lethal Japanese attack. Defeat now might very well paralyze the American war effort against Japan. Still, however unthinkable defeat might be, there seemed little chance the outnumbered Americans could win a victory.

Spruance left his cruiser, *Northampton,* and moved his flag to Halsey's *Enterprise.* With him he took only some luggage and his new flag lieutenant, Robert J. Oliver, an intelligent, irrepressible young man. Oliver was very fond of Spruance. And, though Spruance might have been the last to admit it, he was very fond of Oliver.

When there was brief time ashore Oliver was often the only one Spruance could find to accompany him on his arduous walks and swims. While everyone else scampered off to the officers' club bar, Oliver could be seen striding along the trails and beaches of Oahu with Spruance.

Once on one of their walks Oliver spoke disparagingly of the

Japanese race. Spruance halted and said in effect to his young flag lieutenant, "Now look here, Oliver, if the Japanese are as inferior as you make them out to be, why is that we Americans are so worried whether we're going to beat them in this war?"

Whereas Halsey liked to cry, "Kill Japs, kill Japs, kill Japs!" Spruance was never heard to disparage the enemy. He found the Japanese interesting, intelligent people—worthy enemies. Once, later in the war, he walked up to a group of Japanese prisoners of war and spoke to them through the barbed wire. To the stark incredulity of the American officers with him and the prisoners themselves, Spruance addressed them in a kind of pidgin English, saying they were doing a good job of fighting the war.

Oliver's chief duties as flag lieutenant were to supervise the admiral's communications in flag-hoist, semaphore and flashing light, but he cared so much about Spruance's well-being that he sometimes brooded over him like a mother hen. He had no idea how Spruance had been mollycoddled by his grandmother and aunts when growing up and how fiercely the youth had resisted their fussing over him.

When the task force had been returning from the Tokyo raid the weather turned very cold but Spruance persisted in wearing lightweight khakis to the bridge. Oliver finally had remonstrated with him, saying, "Admiral, it's too cold for you to be up here dressed like that."

Spruance fumed about the bridge for a while, then told his flag lieutenant, "If you want to worry about me, do it when it gets hot! I can stand the cold!"

Oliver was astonished—and puzzled. He had no way of knowing that more than forty years before Spruance had gone into bitter weather thinly dressed and snapped at his scolding grandmother, "I won't be mollycoddled!" *

---

* Buell, *The Quiet Warrior.*

Though Halsey had spoken glowingly of Spruance to his staff officers, they were apprehensive about their new commander. As aviators with undying loyalty to Halsey, they took a dim view of being commanded by a cruiser man. After Spruance came aboard *Enterprise* with his flag lieutenant, the staff members sought out Oliver and asked him what manner of a man was this Spruance. They had heard he was cold, secretive, withdrawn as compared to the open, ebullient Halsey.

"Spruance is the best," Oliver told everyone. "You wait and see."

So he felt chagrined after all assembled in the mess for the first meal with the new admiral. Spruance said not a word until the silence at the long table passed from awkward to painful. Not until coffee was served did Spruance raise his head and speak pleasantly: "Gentlemen, I want you to know that I do not have the slightest concern about any of you. If you were not good, Bill Halsey would not have you."

That thawed the chill. But it was not entirely true of how Spruance felt. He was worried about Halsey's chief of staff, Captain Miles Browning—who in turn was even more apprehensive about Spruance.

Browning, who would be Spruance's chief advisor, had the reputation of being a brilliant naval air tactician. Lean, hawk-faced and sardonic, Browning had made many enemies among the aviators because of his bad temper and emotionally unstable ways. Halsey was the only one who could control Browning; he ignored his instability and wilder ideas but used his wiser suggestions. Spruance knew that Halsey was no administrator and assumed that his chief of staff kept things in order for him. But to his dismay after coming aboard, he found that Browning was no better an administrator than Halsey. The ship's files, for example, were badly disorganized; there was a tendency aboard *Enterprise,* in the words of one pilot, "to fly it by the seat of your pants." Results were what mattered, of course, but to a well organized person like Spruance the disarray was troubling.

Task Force 16 filed out of Pearl Harbor on the morning of May 28, assumed circular formation and shaped course west by northwest under fair skies. Radio silence was to be preserved at all costs. Spruance had composed a message to the force. The signal lamps of *Enterprise* began to clatter, their flashing lights drawing the attention of all ships like a conductor tapping his baton to alert his orchestra. Signalmen on all the other ships blinked their lights to tell *Enterprise* they were listening. Then the signalmen began chanting the words flashing in Morse code from the signal bridge of the flagship. The chanted words were carefully recorded by apprentice signalmen known as strikers. The words were Spruance's:

AN ATTACK FOR THE PURPOSE OF CAPTURING MIDWAY IS EXPECTED. THE ATTACKING FORCE MAY BE COMPOSED OF ALL COMBATANT TYPES INCLUDING FOUR OR FIVE CARRIERS, TRANSPORTS AND TRAIN VESSELS. IF PRESENCE OF TASK FORCE 16 AND 17 REMAINS UNKNOWN TO THE ENEMY WE SHOULD BE ABLE TO MAKE SURPRISE FLANK ATTACKS ON ENEMY CARRIERS FROM A POSITION NORTHEAST OF MIDWAY. . . .

There was a naval tradition that all American leaders engaged in crucial battles should utter a few memorable words for the fighters and for the inspiration of future patriots. There had been some rhetorical ones: "Don't give up the ship! . . ." "I have not yet begun to fight! . . ." "We have met the enemy and they are ours! . . ." "Damn the torpedoes! Full speed ahead! . . ."

Oliver, who gave the message to the signalmen to send, hoped that the admiral would conclude his remarks to the force with something ringing. Spruance probably hoped so too. He was always humbly aware of his lack of eloquence. If Bill Halsey had been sending the message he no doubt would have come up with a memorable sentiment.

Spruance thought and thought. He always had been embarrassed by patriotic declamations. Let deeds speak for themselves. Sometimes words could try too hard and make a speaker sound absurd. The best sentence he could come up with was:

THE SUCCESSFUL CONCLUSION OF THE OPERATION NOW COMMENCING WILL BE OF GREAT VALUE TO OUR COUNTRY.

The mild, awkward words disappointed Oliver. Yet eloquence might have been dishonest, for it would have been out of character for Raymond A. Spruance.

10

Command Decision

The signalmen who sent and received Spruance's messages were doing one of the hundreds of jobs that enlisted men had to perform in order to make a task force function efficiently. The successful prosecution of the war involved far more than smart high command decisions.

Everyone had to depend on everyone else. There were hundreds of parts to the entirety of a combat action. An unfueled plane could not fly, and an unmanned antiaircraft gun could not fire. An engine room was forever staffed, and on a large ship the cooking and consumption of food never ceased. There was no end to the unglamorous and highly important tasks of enlisted men at sea and ashore. Each had to try to be as efficient at his specialty as the surgeon operating in the ship's hospital.

An enlisted man's error could be as costly as a skipper's error of judgment, such as what happened on Midway Atoll while its Navy and Marine garrisons prepared for the coming battle. Near the end of May a demolition test was held. A sailor threw the wrong switch—and 400,000 gallons of aviation gasoline and pumping equipment went up in flames. A half-million gallons remained, but all

Midway-based planes had to be fueled by hand throughout the battle.

It was all very well for Nimitz to say that *Yorktown* must be back in operation in three days, but it took the skilled and tireless efforts of more than 1,400 civilians and naval enlisted men to make it happen. Machinists, welders, electricians, shipwrights, shipfitters poured into Waltzing Matilda. Repairs were not as easy as Nimitz had made them sound. In order to restore the ship's structural strength, deck plates and bulkhead stanchions had to be replaced, as did wiring, fixtures and instruments knocked out by the blast. There was not time for blueprints. Wooden templates of parts which had to be replaced were used as models for steel pieces which were forged into shape and rushed to installation.

Around noon on May 29 the carrier was floated out of drydock with workmen still toiling furiously. Some continued their work until the last moment on the morning of May 30, when *Yorktown* and her escorts sailed under Fletcher to join Spruance.

On the last day of May, while awaiting Fletcher, Spruance's ships were refueled by oilers *Cimarron* and *Platte*. The business of refueling, which seemed so routine, was complicated. A stranger standing on the bridge of *Enterprise* and watching the escort vessels wheel and dart about on the blue, foam-flecked sea would have thought no one knew what he was doing. But the process of fueling each ship in turn while others guarded against submarine or plane attack was choreographed like a ballet. A group commander directed the movements of all ships with signal flags and flashing lights.

The squat oilers labored into the seas while each combat vessel in turn came up fast astern, then slowed to maintain the precise pace of the oiler once abreast of her. Shot lines arced across the open water separating the vessels and were quickly seized. Attached to them were thicker messenger lines, then inhaul lines and span wires. At last straining gangs of crewmen, toiling like seamen in the age of sail, lugged in the thick fuel oil hoses, and boatswain's mates guided the nozzles into the receiving trunks. Then the oilers pumped across the thick, slimy oil which was the life blood of a fighting naval force. The pumping might go on for hours. Meantime signalmen on the adjoining vessels talked back and forth by moving their hands in semaphore. In times of peace the band of a large man o' war sometimes serenaded the oiler men—but that was not happening as Task Force 16 prepared for the Battle of Midway.

Combat marines and infantrymen liked to say that the sailors of the fleet led an easy life. That was not so. It was true that living was cleaner aboard ship than in the foxholes, and the food supply generally was more stable. In times of calm when things were running on schedule a sailor had four hours on duty and then eight hours off. That changed in combat, of course, when everyone usually was too charged up to sleep even if he had the chance.

Though a ship was cleaner than a tent in mud, it afforded no privacy. World War II duty aboard a submarine has been likened to living in a phone booth and the lot of a destroyer man to being stuck on a racing roller coaster. So life aboard an aircraft carrier could be compared to dwelling in a rush-hour Grand Central Terminal. Noise, a restless din, was every man's constant companion. In time it told on one's nerves. To some men on sea duty the threat of being attacked was worse than attack itself. For some it was worse to live with the fear of being trapped below than to be one of an antiaircraft gun crew on the open decks. There was no place to hide from bombs and torpedoes.

Good officers like Nimitz and Spruance understood that the monotony of long weeks at sea in confined quarters and the tensions of combat made it essential for men to have shore liberty as often as possible. When Nimitz sent *Yorktown* off toward Midway after its long weeks at sea he did it regretfully, promising its officers and men that when they returned to Pearl he would send the carrier back to the West Coast for a thorough refurbishing that would give everyone extensive shore leave.

*   *   *

The one person aboard *Enterprise* who could find solitude was Spruance. He seems to have been one of those rare and fortunate persons who never had any problems with loneliness. He ate most of his meals alone and passed nearly all of his time either in his cabin or on the open flag bridge atop the island, as the carrier's superstructure high above the flight deck was called. From this eagle's aerie he could sweep the horizon and watch the configurations of his force. The details of Task Force 16's daily operations he left to others so that he had freedom to concentrate on coming events.

Spruance had a plan which he had discussed at a council of war with Nimitz and Fletcher on May 27. Basically it was a simple plan: he wanted to hit the enemy carriers before they struck him—hit them quickly and hard with all his available strength and with the intent of sinking them. Only after he sank the carriers—and if he had any air strength left—would he go after the escorting battleships and cruisers.

Serious risks were involved in his plan of committing his entire force of planes in a massive attack and holding nothing in reserve. If he caught the enemy unawares and demolished their carriers, the Japanese would be unable to retaliate. If, however, the enemy planes found his carriers first, their overwhelming numbers would crush the Americans.

Buell writes in his absorbing biography *The Quiet Warrior,* "Spruance knew he would need luck as well as surprise in order to win. Critics later called him cautious, saying that he lacked boldness and was not aggressive. They were wrong. His plan was bold and daring. He was going for the Japanese jugular."

Of course surprise was essential to Spruance's plan. Therefore he ordered strict radio silence for Task Force 16—not even any short-range Talk Between Ships. The silence was not to be broken, he said, even to bring home a lost plane.

After refueling his ships on May 31 Spruance took up the station Nimitz had assigned about 325 miles northeast of Midway. There

Fletcher joined him with *Yorktown* and her screen of cruisers and destroyers on the afternoon of June 2. Both task forces had avoided detection by enemy submarines, which were late in reaching their patrolling grounds.

After the two forces rendezvoused Fletcher assumed tactical command of the operation. According to the developing theory of sea-air warfare with aircraft carriers, it was best to keep flattops apart and maneuvering independently. So Fletcher ordered Spruance to operate his Task Force 16 about ten miles to the south of his own Task Force 17. This kept the two far enough apart but still within visual signalling distance while maintaining strict radio silence. For the coming battle the attack planes would be launched from Spruance's carriers *Enterprise* and *Hornet*. Fletcher's *Yorktown* would provide search planes and defensive fighters. These were called CAP, for Combat Air Patrol. Fletcher ordered Spruance to be ready to launch the attack planes on brief notice.

The tactical commander of the carrier forces was answerable to Nimitz and had no control over the land-based planes and defense units on Midway. These, operating independently of the admirals at sea, also were answerable only to Nimitz. Neither did the tactical commander of the carriers have any say over the actions of the American submarines involved.

The submarines were deployed basically as scouts rather than being grouped as a tactical threat to the attacking enemy forces.

A total of 15 boats were engaged under the command of Rear Amiral Robert H. English, Commander Submarines Pacific Fleet, at Pearl Harbor. Twelve of these submarines were assigned patrol stations west of Midway. The 3 others patrolled a scouting line between Midway and Oahu. Reports of their observations and actions were radioed to English and passed along to Nimitz. Hypo was feeding English relevant signal intelligence about the Japanese which was passed along when required in his orders to the fleet boats. Thus, in respect to submarines as well as all other areas of American strength, Nimitz exercised strong central authority. He was, in effect, present at the scene in every way but physically.

Yorktown launched its searches for the enemy early on the morning of June 3. The wait was tense aboard *Enterprise,* and everyone felt the same aboard *Hornet,* which was commanded by Captain Marc A. Mitscher. There was a growing wonder whether Nimitz's forecast of enemy plans and intentions could have been wrong. If the Japanese had worked an elaborate ruse and now were on the way to attack Pearl Harbor, the main strength of the American fleet had been drawn into an absurd position where it could inflict no damage on the enemy.

But then in midmorning of June 3 Midway patrol planes sighted the anticipated invasion force about 700 miles west-southwest of the atoll. Since it was almost precisely where Nimitz's Hypo intelligence had forecast it would be at that time, maybe CINCPAC was also right about the striking force of four or more carriers coming down from the northwest on Midway. Fletcher ordered Task Forces 16 and 17 to move slowly south to be in a closer intercept position.

Spruance prowled the flag bridge restlessly most of June 3, waiting. Up there Halsey had established a command post known as the flag shelter. Its furniture consisted of a chart table, a voice radio handset, sound-powered phone outlets, a couple of uncomfortable Navy-issue settees and some metal book racks containing old tactical publications.

Wherever Spruance went on *Enterprise* he carried a rolled up 20-inch-square maneuvering board—a paper form containing compass rose and distance scale which mariners use to solve relative motion problems at sea. Staff officers wondered why the admiral always kept it with him.

One of the chief things Spruance and Fletcher were watching as they waited on their ships that June 3 was the weather chart. About 300 to 400 miles northwest of Midway there was almost always fog where the trade winds struck the Japan Current. Especially in May and June the area often was crossed by storms which were preceded by weather fronts of clouds and rain. That was precisely the situation on June 3: a wide band of fog and showers stretched across the seas northwest of Midway. The American ships were moving slowly in a high pressure area of bright sunlight. But what did the clouds and showers to the northwest hide? Search planes from Midway could not find anything in the murk. Nevertheless, Fletcher remembered how Japanese men of war had hidden from him under the band of clouds in the Coral Sea.

Admiral Nagumo, victor at Pearl Harbor, flew his flag aboard *Akagi,* pride of the Japanese carrier fleet, as commander of the Japanese striking force descending on Midway from the northwest. He felt calm and confident as his ships prowled slowly toward their initial target under the cover of thick clouds and fog.

A couple of times the Japanese, hearing the drone of airplane engines, knew they were listening to American Midway-based planes which could not see them. There was no indication that American naval vessels were anywhere in the area. Commander Minoru Genda, the foremost Japanese air tactician, who had been assigned to Nagumo's staff, was of the opinion the Americans' weak carrier forces had been drawn off by the Japanese move against the Aleutians. Nagumo believed Genda, who was reputed never to be wrong in his estimates; Genda was, in fact, the one person for whose safety the great Yamamoto had expressed concern in the coming battle. Nagumo may have thought it would have been pleasant if Yamamoto had expressed a bit of concern about Nagumo himself; failing that, however, it was good to have the benefit of Genda's genius aboard *Akagi.*

Nagumo's orders were on June 4 to "execute an aerial attack on Midway . . . destroying all enemy forces stationed there" with the planes of his four big carriers. This would soften up the defenses for the landing force coming from Guam and Saipan, which was scheduled to invade Midway on June 5. The high command was so certain of victory that it even had provided the conquerors with a new

Japanese name for Midway: "Glorious Month of June." * After the conquest of the atoll Nagumo's ships would be refueled and then be ready to take on whatever ragtag forces the overwhelmed Americans might send against them. Nagumo was grateful for the cloud cover that kept his force hidden from American planes. Using this cover had been one of the basic elements in Yamamoto's elaborate plans.

On the morning of June 4, while it was still dark, planes revved up on the decks of *Akagi, Kaga, Hiryu* and *Soryu.* At 0430, when Nagumo's fleet was 240 miles northwest of Midway, the planes began taking off from the carriers. By 0500 the Midway attack was launched: 36 Kate torpedo planes and 36 Val dive-bombers escorted by 36 Zeke fighters were winging through dawn's light toward their target.

Spruance was awake as early as Nagumo. Accompanied by Oliver, he climbed to the flag bridge. There they were joined by Browning and other staff officers.

Tension grew as they waited and listened to incoherent fragments on the Midway radio frequencies. Twice the *Enterprise* pilots manned their planes on false alarms, and both times they were called back to the ready rooms. Fletcher on *Yorktown* was being very alert and watchful. He was worried that the Japanese might slip past the Americans and head for Pearl Harbor. Just before dawn he sent ten planes off on a search to the north on the chance the Hypo intelligence had been wrong and the Japanese striking force was coming out of the northeast rather than the northwest.

Suddenly, at 0534, the voice of a Midway search pilot hawked out of the static: "Enemy carriers!"

But where? And how many were they?

The officers on the flag bridge moved about nervously, dragging

*Morison, *History of United States Naval Operations in World War II*, Vol. 4.

on cigarettes and listening for a meaningful message to emerge from the static.

At 0545 a search pilot reported numerous enemy planes 150 miles from Midway and approaching from the northwest. But where were the enemy carriers *precisely?*

At 0603 the same voice squawked from the loudspeaker again: "Two carriers with battleships bearing 320, distance 180, course 135, speed 24."

Chief of Staff Miles Browning and the other officers sprang to the navigation chart like a gang of excited children. As all grabbed for the measuring dividers, the watch officer stabbed a finger with one of its sharp points. He yelped: first casualty in the Battle of Midway.

Oliver watched Spruance intently as the admiral unrolled his maneuvering board. The flag lieutenant had wondered what it contained but had not felt free to ask. Now he saw to his surprise that it was blank—not even a pencil mark.

After the staff swiftly plotted the reported enemy position, Spruance said, "Read me the contact report."

Someone did.

"Is it authenticated?"

"Yes sir."

"Now give me the ranges and bearings from Midway to the enemy and to us."

By plotting these on his maneuvering board, he could measure the distance from Task Force 16 to the enemy. Using his thumb and index finger as dividers, he estimated the distance as about 175 miles. That was within the maximum range of his torpedo planes.

Spruance rolled up his maneuvering board and said, "Launch the attack!" It was 0615.

In making his fateful command decision, in taking that big gamble, there were many things Spruance did not know.

One of these, a thing not even the codebreakers knew, was that Admiral Yamamoto himself was present for the battle. Behind the striking force and the landing force there was yet a third Japanese force composed of 7 battleships, 1 light carrier, 3 light cruisers, 21 destroyers. Yamamoto was aboard the chief of these to the west of Midway. It was an extraordinary battleship called *Yamato*, the largest warship ever built. Displacing about 59,000 tons and so heavily armored that it was impervious to any American air or naval weapon of the time, *Yamato* mounted nine 18-inch guns—more firepower than any ship in history.

11

Confusion

Though the Midway search pilot had reported only two carriers, Spruance believed Hypo's intelligence that four were in the enemy force advancing from the northwest. Since the wind was blowing from Midway toward the enemy fleet, the Japanese obviously would continue to approach the atoll in order to recover their first launch, which—the radio traffic indicated—had already been made against the garrison there. Once the enemy carriers had refueled and rearmed their aircraft, their next launch no doubt would be against the American task force after it was discovered. And it seemed inevitable that enemy search planes would find them at any moment.

That was why Spruance had decided he must not wait. He must gamble on the Japanese carriers all being together and strike with his full strength at once. If all the carriers were not together, he would have launched his total strength against only a part of the enemy, who well might destroy him in return. But he must take the risk.

He planned a coordinated attack with *Enterprise* and *Hornet* air groups flying together and then each attacking one Japanese carrier. Dive-bombers would hurtle on the enemy from above while torpedo bombers skimmed the surface. Both would be protected from the enemy CAP (Combat Air Patrol) by fighter escorts.

After Spruance ordered the attack launched, the sweat was on Browning, who had to make complicated calculations from many variables: the relative motion of the two forces; the chance the reported enemy position was wrong; wind velocity and direction; the fuel capacity, endurance and combat radius of the planes; the time lapse between launchings of planes; the time necessary for sending the attack order to *Hornet* by flashing light. *Enterprise* sounded General Quarters and the force turned west with speed stepped up to 20 knots; Fletcher remained behind with *Yorktown* to recover search planes.

Spruance accepted Browning's recommendation of an 0700 launch time. At that hour the carrier turned bow into the light southeast wind and speeded up to 25 knots with the plan of launching 64 planes in 30 minutes. As the attack began, the ship seemed to explode with almost unendurable noise. From the flight deck rose the roar of engines as pilot after pilot gunned his craft while the loudspeaker in the flag shelter blared orders. Officers and signalmen bounded about like puppets dancing to invisible strings, and off-stage voices seemed to shout at one another. Above the dissonance and flurry the admiral stood quietly, a graven figure of calm concentration, his tensions tightly belted in his gut.

Browning, on the other hand, felt a need to release his tensions with leaps and shouts, like a child playing war in a back yard. Spruance instinctively mistrusted people who acted so, but there was nothing he could do about it now. The outlook was not auspicious— and grew worse steadily.

Spruance had assigned Oliver the task of timing and counting the takeoff of planes. The flight deck gave a different perspective to the frenzy; it was a scene Oliver never would forget. The crews came up from the ready rooms, where intelligence officers had given them a final briefing. Their faces were boyish in growing morning light and each showed a fringe of unshaven peach fuzz; it was their ritual not to shave until a battle was ended—a ritual joined in for once by the meticulously groomed Spruance. The flight crews' close buddies, the ground crews, had finished checking, arming, fueling and servicing the planes. The pilots climbed in casually. Nonchalance was the order of the day: no good for a man to betray nervousness or tension, very bad form. They warmed their engines while planes that already had taken off swooped around *Enterprise* like graceful gulls. There was hand-signalling to the deck directors, a casual wave to your wingman whom you might never see again. And then *go* to join the formation overhead—and soon, perhaps, the heavenly feathered choir. Upstairs the air was fresh and cold; looking down, you saw the wakes of ships streaming like the tails of racing white horses.

To Oliver down below the show went on as precisely mannered as a ballet—maybe a death dance, it was so slow.

By 0730 only 32 planes had been launched, despite Browning's promises, threats and shouts, and these circled overhead wasting precious fuel while waiting for the coordinated attack to shape up.

At 0731 an enemy search plane spotted them, and Spruance realized they had lost the advantage of surprise. At 0745, with the torpedo planes still not launched, he abandoned his plan of a coordinated operation and signalled the *Enterprise* air group commander, Lieutenant Commander Clarence W. McClusky, to go ahead and attack with the bombers then aloft. Not until 0806 did the last torpedo bomber thunder off the deck.

Then Spruance ordered the force to come about and close the enemy at top speed of 25 knots. He believed that the Japanese fleet must have been alerted to his presence and changed course, so it no longer would be where he had sent his airmen.

Suddenly there was nothing to do but wait for news that surely could only be bad.

Nagumo's 108 carrier-based planes honed in on Midway in tight V-formations with an umbrella of Zeke fighters overhead. The Midway Marine Corps fighter squadron rose gallantly to meet them, but it was totally outclassed in equipment, if not in fighting heart.

The marines flew 20 antique Buffaloes, which were as fond of wallowing as their bison namesake, and six old Wildcats, which some pilots referred to as Wilbur Wrights. They were no match for the swift Zekes. The marine fighters climbed laboriously to 17,000 feet; they intended to swoop down on the Japanese like planes in a World War I movie. But their craft responded so heavily and slowly that nearly every marine fighter came out of the fray with one to five Zekes on his tail. The marines shot down a surprising number of the enemy, but they were riddled. Of the 26 fighters, 17 were destroyed and 7 others damaged severely.

The principal aim of the Japanese bombers was to knock out the main Midway airstrip. They destroyed the Marine Corps command post, mess hall, seaplane hangar and the oil tanks on Sand Island; they set fire to the powerhouse on Eastern Island, the hospital and storehouses. But they killed very few men on the ground, and they failed to make the runways unusable.

Meantime Midway-based bombers were going after the Japanese carriers approaching from the northwest. They found them at 0710, but they were shot down left and right by enemy fighters. One of two B-26s which made it back to Midway was repaired and flew next day to Pearl Harbor. There the pilot told a tall tale of sinking a Japanese carrier. It was the first news the American public had of the battle, and—like so much first news in war—it was badly in error.

After sending his force against the land defenses of Midway, Nagumo reserved 108 planes—36 dive-bombers, 36 torpedo bombers, 36 fighters—to use armor-piercing bombs and torpedoes against any American ships which might be found. Following a report of an American carrier, Nagumo made a fateful decision. It was then a bit after 0830 and the Japanese planes which had attacked Midway were returning, short on fuel. Also in the air and running low on gas were the remaining fighters which were protecting their carriers. Nagumo faced a choice: He could (1) launch the bombers on deck and send them against the Americans without fighter escort, or (2) recover his fighters and Midway attackers and rearm them.

Yamaguchi, second in command, recommended an immediate attack. Genda advised recovering the planes in the air. Nagumo took Genda's advice. At 0837 the four Japanese carriers turned into the wind, flying signal flags ordering the planes to land.

The concentration of the Japanese on their job was not helped by harassment from 16 Midway-based Marine Corps dive-bombers piloted by brave and inexperienced young men. They glided rather than dived on their targets, which definitely was not the thing to do against fighter and AA opposition. Eight were shot down, and the six that made it back to the base never could be flown again. One pilot, Lieutenant Daniel Iverson USMC, had his microphone shot off his neck and his Dauntless took *259* hits. The plane was a total wreck, but Iverson emerged unscathed—much to his surprise.

Next, 15 Flying Fortresses passed over the Japanese fleet, each bomber dropping 8500 pounds of bombs from 20,000 feet—too high an altitude for the Zekes to reach them. Despite extravagant claims, these B-17s scored no better than near-misses on Nagumo's force. Nimitz had been skeptical about the ability of high-level bombers to hit moving sea targets. Experience proved him right: high-altiude bombing of ships by any of the armed forces never was effective throughout the war.

After the Flying Forts turned back to Midway, 11 Marine Corps scout bombers came in. They lost two and did no damage to the Japanese.

Ineffective as were these American assaults, they were a distraction to the Japanese at a crucial time when they were frantically receiving and rearming their planes and when every moment counted.

At that point the Japanese clearly had won the first round of the battle. For a loss of about 40 planes they had destroyed half the

Midway-based aircraft and inflicted great damage to the atoll's installations.

After *Enterprise* and *Hornet* had launched their planes into the fickle wind, they began to close the estimated position of the enemy. They did not know Nagumo had changed course by ninety degrees and was hunting *them*.

Yorktown followed them leisurely, keeping a distance. She had launched a strike group of 35 planes by 0906 and had another deck-load ready for action. Fletcher was being prudent by saving planes for an emergency. No doubt he remembered how a faulty sighting report in the Battle of the Coral Sea had made him go all out for little *Shoho* and so miss bigger game.

To Spruance and his officers on the flag bridge of *Enterprise* the wait was excruciating. Nothing came from the loudspeaker but static and occasional unintelligible fragments of pilots' talk. Perhaps it was as well that they did not know what was happening.

Nagumo's 4 carriers were in a boxlike formation inside a protective screen of 2 battleships, 3 cruisers and 11 destroyers. It was at 0917, after the carriers had recovered all of the Midway raiders, that this big force made its 90-degree turn and sailed east-northeast in search of the American ships. Rearming and refueling of the planes continued frenetically.

Nagumo's change of course resulted in the dive-bombers from *Hornet* missing his force entirely. When Commander Stanhope C. Ring, *Hornet* attack group commander, failed to find the enemy at the anticipated place, he turned his 35 dive-bombers and fighter cover on a Midway bearing and thus flew in the opposite direction from the Japanese. All the fighters ran out of fuel and had to ditch in the sea, 13 bombers landed at Midway for gas, two splashed into the lagoon there and everyone missed the battle.

The 15 planes of the *Hornet* torpedo squadron, led by Lieutenant Commander John C. Waldron, became separated from Ring's high-flying dive-bombers by a cloud cover soon after takeoff. Then in the confusion the fighters from *Enterprise* joined up with the 15 *Hornet* torpedo bombers, thinking they also were from *Enterprise*. When Waldron did not find the enemy carriers where they were supposed to be, he turned north—while Ring, out of communication with Waldron, had turned south toward Midway. Soon Waldron and his pilots saw columns of smoke on the horizon. Swerving toward it, they found the Japanese fleet spread out before them.

Waldron still had fighter protection but did not know it. Lieutenant J. S. Gray's *Enterprise* fighter squadron, which had mistakenly accompanied him at the outset, had disappeared. Waldron probably thought they had realized their mistake and gone looking for *Enterprise* bombers. But Gray still believed that Waldron's squadron was the *Enterprise* torpedo unit commanded by Lieutenant Commander Eugene E. Lindsey. According to a prearranged plan with Lindsey, Gray took his fighters high to 19,000 feet, where Waldron could not see them. Lindsey then was to call him down for protection against Zekes when he took his squadron in for attack. Of course Waldron knew nothing about this arrangement. So the signal never came, and Gray did not come down.

Though lacking fighter protection and though enemy Zekes hovered like a swarm of wasps ready to pounce on them, the torpedo bombers led by Waldron lumbered in heavily at low altitude. The Japanese antiaircraft fire was so intense it seared faces and tore chunks out of planes. And then the Zekes dived on them. Still the heavy old Devastators rumbled on toward the southernmost carrier.

Waldron, seeing that this carrier was protected by an impenetrable barrage of AA fire, changed his squadron's course toward the center carrier. As more Zekes came screaming down with guns blazing, Ensign George H. Gay saw the planes ahead launching their torpedoes. Then one ... two ... three burst into flames and began breaking up. It never occurred to Gay to deviate from course. He had been trained to attack, which maybe was as good a way as any to learn to accept death, and he had no intention of doing anything else as the entire right wing of a plane flipped past him.

The insanity, however, was not in the way the bombers were being blown apart but how the torpedoes were not detonating. Something had to be wrong with the cursed torpedoes, as everybody said.

Gay dropped his torpedo and pulled out sharply ten feet above the carrier's deck. As he swerved his plane into the wake of the carrier, an exploding shell from a pursuing Zeke carried away his left rudder control and something like dry ice enveloped his left arm. His radio man already was dead, and Gay was sure he was about to join him. He knew he would have to ditch, but there was no time to do it gracefully. His Devastator plowed into the sea with the force of a ten-ton truck smashing into a stone wall.

An invisible fist dealt Gay a mighty sock that made him struggle for consciousness. He sank and died and rose, still struggling for consciousness. Suddenly he won the struggle. He was alive, treading water and clutching for the rubber boat in its bag, which had floated clear of his plane's wreckage. Finally regaining the sense to inflate his jacket, Gay grabbed hold of the boat bag with his wounded left hand, which felt asleep. With his right hand he snatched a black cushion which had blown out of the bomber compartment and held it over him so that enemy gunners could not see his precious American head.

All 15 *Hornet* torpedo bombers had been destroyed. All 30 of their crewmen were dead except for Ensign Gay, who floated with a precarious hold on life. He had a soggy ringside view of what happened next in one of the crucial battles of World War II.

What happened was that the *Enterprise* torpedo squadron led by Lindsey found and struck Nagumo's fleet. Lindsey led his planes in as bravely as Waldron had, and the destruction was resumed. Within minutes 10 of the 14 Devastators were shot down.

Gray and his *Enterprise* fighters still hovered high above. Possibly Lindsey did not call them down for protection because he did not know they were there. Possibly Gray did not understand how crucial the action was. There was a mammoth failure in American communications—maybe mechanical, but more likely human. If Gray, Waldron or Lindsey notified their carriers at this stage that they had sighted the enemy fleet, word never reached Spruance or Fletcher.

Still devastation day for Devastators continued. The Japanese had scarcely disposed of the *Enterprise* squadron when they were discovered and attacked by the *Yorktown* torpedo squadron under Lieutenant Commander Lance E. Massey. These bombers were accompanied by a half-dozen Wildcat fighters. A swarm of Zekes bagged the Wildcats, then sent seven Devastators, including Massey's, crashing down in flames.

The best that could be said for the Americans at that juncture was that a number of young men who had been reared to hate war were fighting with magnificent bravery.

Another round clearly had gone to the Japanese. Of 41 torpedo bombers from the American carriers, all but 6 had been destroyed. And not a single American torpedo had touched the enemy ships.

Yet there is no substitute for bravery in war. The fearless actions of the torpedo pilots had worked subtle effects on the Japanese. The clever maneuvering and swift evasive actions of Nagumo's carriers in their efforts to avoid being torpedoed had made it impossible for them to launch any planes. And the torpedo plane attacks had brought the Zekes down to deck level when they should have been above, forming a high protective umbrella.

On *Enterprise* taut nerves were close to snapping over the lack of firm information.

Air group commander McClusky and his dive-bombers from *Enterprise* had been hunting the enemy fleet since 0752. When he reached the point where he had expected to see it there was nothing but empty ocean. Thinking the enemy might have turned to the southwest, he flew 35 miles in that direction before turning north at 0935. Twenty minutes later, while flying at 19,000 feet, McClusky saw a

Japanese destroyer speeding into the northeast. He correctly assumed she was trying to catch up to Nagumo's force and turned his dive-bombers in that direction.

Now, strategy having failed, chance began to put togther the parts of battle. At 0952 the wandering Gray radioed McClusky that he was running low on gas and would have to go home soon. Perhaps he saw McClusky's formation of dive-bombers at last—perhaps he was just making a formal report to his commander somewhere in the wild blue yonder. In any event, the officers clustered in the flag shelter of *Enterprise* heard him.

And then, at 1000, Gray finally reported the presence and course of half of Nagumo's force: two carriers, two battleships and eight destroyers heading north without air cover.

This was the first Spruance or Fletcher knew that the enemy force had been sighted.

On *Enterprise* the excitable Browning leaped to the microphone and cried, "Attack! Attack!"

The next voice heard over the flag shelter's loudspeaker was McClusky's: "Wilco, as soon as I find the bastards."

After more agonizing minutes McClusky cried, "Tally ho!" It meant he had found the enemy and was going in for the kill.

There followed his crisp orders to the commanders of his two squadrons of Dauntless dive-bombers. He told Lieutenant W. E. Gallaher's squadron to follow him in attacking *Kaga*. Lieutenant R. H. Best's squadron he told to take care of *Akagi*. Gallaher's bombers were armed only with 500-pound bombs, because they had been launched from *Enterprise* so early that there had not been sufficient flight deck space for a heavily armed plane to take off. Best's planes, launched later, carried half-ton bombs.

The squadrons tipped over and came screaming down at a 70-degree angle, speeds rising to 335 miles per hour. The Japanese were taken completely by surprise. They were straightening course after ducking and weaving from the previous torpedo attacks and their

Zekes were just beginning to climb toward combat altitude when the bombs struck the carriers like sledgehammers on undefended heads. So great was the surprise that scarcely an AA gun was fired at them.

At last, in that morning of confusion and error, luck was good to the Americans. By mistake, Best's second division of three planes launched its half-ton bombs at *Kaga*. So both carriers received a lethal dose.

Yet the American string of good luck still had not run out. At almost the moment McClusky found and attacked the enemy, Lieutenant Commander M. F. Leslie of *Yorktown* struck *Soryu* with 17 dive-bombers. He had left home at 0906, later than the *Enterprise* and *Hornet* planes, and had been smarter about finding the enemy. When he came to the line connecting the last reported position of the carriers with Midway, he led his bombers up its reverse away from the atoll. After sighting smoke in the sky, he found the enemy fleet. He caught up with both McClusky and *Yorktown*'s torpedo planes under Massey. The plan called for Leslie to go in first with his dive-bombers. But Massey, ignoring the plan, impetuously went ahead of him with his torpedo bombers—and was destroyed. As is obvious, sheer coincidence rather than planning brought Leslie to the target at the same time as McClusky.

Leslie's bombers began their dive from 14,500 feet with the morning sun at their backs. They hurtled down in three waves, one coming on *Soryu* from the starboard bow, another from the starboard quarter and the third from the port quarter. Within three minutes three lethal hits were made with half-ton bombs.

Newly armed and fueled planes were spotted for takeoff on the flight deck when the Americans struck. One bomb went through the forward deck and exploded in the hangar below, folding up the elevator like an accordion. The second hit amidships and the third near the after elevator, turning the entire ship into a sheet of flames. As last seen, Captain Yanagimoto was standing on the bridge crying "Banzai!" while flames enveloped him.

While *Hiryu* escaped unscathed to the north with some surface vessels, fires raged and terror reigned on *Kaga* and *Akagi*. Like *Soryu,* they were in the highest possible state of vulnerability to attack. Their flight decks bore an armed and fueled force ready to take off while a second strike force was being prepared below. Discarded bombs lying around hangar decks awaiting stowage in the magazines went off like firecrackers in the general holocaust. On *Akagi* the fires also started torpedoes exploding.

Nagumo's blunt-speaking chief of staff, Rear Admiral Kusaka, later told American interrogators that "There was a terrific fire aboard ship that was just like hell."*

Nagumo refused to come down from the bridge when told the carrier must be abandoned, probably from a sense of duty to remain with his flagship. Kusaka pleaded with him, but Nagumo was adamant. At last Kusaka and other officers dragged him away. They had to lower themselves by ropes from the bridge since the ladders were ablaze.

"When I got down," Kusaka recalled, "the deck was on fire and antiaircraft and machine guns were firing automatically, having been set off by fire. Bodies were all over the place, and it wasn't possible to tell what would be shot up next. . . . That is eventually the way we abandoned the *Akagi*—helter-skelter, no order of any kind."

Kusaka, hands and feet burned, Nagumo and other staff officers were transferred to the cruiser *Nagara*. Every Japanese command warship bore a portrait of the emperor, which was considered sacred; the ritual of rescuing Hirohito's picture from *Akagi* and moving it to *Nagara* was completed late in the afternoon.

Miraculously, within a few minutes, badly disorganized American air squadrons had destroyed three of Japan's most powerful carriers. But could the Americans, greatly outnumbered by enemy surface ships, hope for more than a draw in this crucial battle?

---

* Morison, *History of United States Naval Operations in World War II,* Vol. 4.

12

Pursuer or Pursued?

Late in the morning of June 4 the American pilots who had survived the attack on the enemy were winging back to their carriers. Some were wounded, some planes were damaged, all planes were short of fuel.

Naturally, an aircraft carrier is constantly moving while its plane crews are absent on missions. A pilot must know his carrier's position when he returns, a navigational reference called Point Option. It is the duty of a command staff to predict a carrier's movements and give pilots the Point Option for their homing. If there is any drastic change in a previously announced position, pilots must be informed by radio.

In the chaotic June 4 morning launching from *Enterprise,* Browning failed to broadcast Point Option. The pilots had been trained to understand that if it was not broadcast before takeoff it meant that the carrier would close the enemy at high speed; on the basis of that knowledge, each pilot would compute his own navigational reference in returning. But the need to speed away frequently into the capricious southeast wind to launch and receive planes had prevented *Enterprise* from closing the enemy as the pilots had been led to believe was happening.

When pilots could not find the carrier at the anticipated location, they began radioing frantically. The staff communicator replied quickly with the carrier's position, but several planes never made it and some landed with as little as five gallons of gas. Spruance was grieved and angered for the unnecessary loss of lives and planes. He blamed Browning for the bad staff work, but as usual kept his feeling to himself.

The pilots who did return swarmed up the ladders of the island to report to the admiral and his staff, their youthful, unshaven faces stained with sweat and oil. Not one complained of the problems and ordeals that had resulted form erratic staff work. Rather, their faces shone through the grime and they shouted out great news as everyone on the high deck was washed by roar after deafening roar of returning planes and the acrid stench of exhaust engulfed them.

"There were four carriers—not three! . . . No, I didn't say that, sir, I said we *hit* three and left 'em burning! . . . That's right. One still out there untouched. . . ."

Suddenly the loudspeaker blared a *Yorktown* report that she was under attack by enemy aircraft. Neither *Enterprise* nor *Hornet* could go to her aid because they were still recovering planes, but Spruance sent two cruisers and two destroyers.

It was just before noon that *Yorktown*'s radar picked up 30 to 40 planes approaching from the northwest at a distance of 40 miles. They were from *Hiryu,* the remaining carrier of Nagumo's force that had not been touched.

Aboard *Yorktown* Admiral Fletcher's flag lieutenant told him, "The attack is coming in, sir."

"Well," replied Fletcher, bent over a chart to figure out his next move and not bothering to glance up, "I've got on my tin hat. I can't do anything else now."

Protective measures were taken swiftly. Returning planes were waved off, fuel lines were drained and filled with carbon dioxide, CAP went up and Waltzing Matilda began her ponderous evasive dance with all AA batteries manned.

Bad luck. A Val, disintegrating under AA fire, let fall a bomb which tumbled onto *Yorktown*'s flight deck, killing many men and starting fires below. These were quickly extinguished by the sprinkler system and water curtains. Then another bomb exploded in the smokestack, rupturing the boilers' uptakes and snuffing out fires. A third hit close to the magazines, which were promptly flooded. These explosions badly damaged communications.

At 1315 Fletcher transferred his flag to cruiser *Astoria*. But he could not direct an air battle from a cruiser. After a time he signalled Spruance: WILL CONFORM TO YOUR MOVEMENTS. What did the vaguely worded signal mean? Spruance correctly decided it meant that Fletcher had passed command of Task Forces 16 and 17 to Spruance.

Meanwhile Browning was beseeching Spruance to launch an attack against *Hiryu*. But the admiral decided to wait. *Yorktown* planes were now beginning to land on both *Enterprise* and *Hornet*. Spruance needed time to get organized. In light of the staff's morning performance there was every reason to believe another hasty attack would become a wild goose chase.

In midafternoon the staff reported both carriers ready to launch, but still Spruance waited. A second attack on *Yorktown,* this time by torpedo planes, had destroyed her electrical power; she was burning badly and appeared finished despite the valiant efforts of damage-control parties. And then a scout plane reported *Hiryu* and escorts 110 miles to the west.

"Launch the attack," Spruance told Browning, "and order *Hornet* to launch."

The staff bumbled along as badly as in the morning. Thirty minutes after receiving the enemy position someone signalled *Hornet* that Spruance didn't know where the enemy was. That message was corrected and the enemy position given, but no one had yet thought to order *Hornet* to launch; everyone believed someone else had done it. When *Enterprise* turned into the wind and began launching 24 bombers, Mitscher, watching from *Hornet,* wondered aloud what was going on and why he had received no orders. Eventually the orders were signalled to him, but through no fault of his own he was late in launching.

Ten of the 24 bombers *Enterprise* launched were from *Yorktown* struck *Hiryu* at 1700, scoring four hits which started uncontrollable fires on the carrier. Three of the dive-bombers were destroyed in the attack. A group of 16 dive-bombers from *Hornet,* arriving late at the scene, went after the cruiser escorts but did no better than near-misses.

Neither Spruance, Nimitz nor anyone else on the American side yet realized that the great Yamamoto, aboard the superbattleship *Yamato,* was a couple of hundred miles to the west of the battle area. (They would not learn that until months later.) With *Yamato* were two other of Japan's newest battleships, adept night fighters, a light carrier and other vessels.

Hypo had failed to learn anything about this force or about Yamamoto's personal participation at Midway because he and this group of vessels had been in the Inland Sea of Japan during the preparations. This command had steamed to Midway under radio silence; no messages were exchanged, and there was nothing for Hypo to intercept.

It was Yamamoto's hope to use the *Yamato* group with the other forces to draw the Americans into a crucial naval battle in the course of taking Midway. Naturally the Japanese Commander in Chief was deeply disturbed by Nagumo's loss of three carriers. But then his spirits picked up when he learned that *Hiryu*'s planes had attacked and presumably sunk *Yorktown.* He ordered two carriers that had attacked Dutch Harbor in Alaska and their screening force to come down and rendezvous at 0900 on June 5 in preparation for a major fleet action. He also ordered Admiral Kondo, supporting the Midway landing force, to bring his powerful ships to join in the action.

But then word came that *Hiryu* had been knocked out and was expected to sink soon.

"The game is up, thought everybody on *Yamato*'s bridge." The words are from Yamamoto's yeoman, who talked to American intelligence officers after the war.* "The members of the staff, their mouths tight shut, looked at one another. . . . indescribable emptiness, cheerlessness and chagrin. . . ."

At last Yamamoto asked, "Is Genda all right?" He was the one officer Yamamoto thought essential to recovery of air power. He had been one of those rescued before *Akagi* went down. But if Genda had genius as a naval air officer, he had not displayed it that day. His bad advice, to recover planes before launching the attack, was the main cause of the Japanese defeat.

After the war he said that he had been worried about his pilot friends who were running low on gas and would have to ditch in the sea unless they refueled quickly. Ruefully he remarked that he had been thinking at the time as a pilot rather than a commander.

By 1915 on that evening Yamamoto had pulled himself together enough to send all division commanders a kind of cheerio message urging attack on the enemy. But Nagumo could not be rallied. He had had it. There were none of the easy joys of the Pearl Harbor raid for him at Midway. A man in his state of mind likes to have his fears confirmed, and so he passed along to Yamamoto at 2130 a really wild report from a cruiser float plane: "The total strength of the enemy is 5 carriers, 6 cruisers and 15 destroyers. These are steaming westward. . . ."

A little more than an hour later Nagumo sent another message that sounded irrational: "There still exist 4 enemy carriers . . . 6 cruisers and 16 destroyers. These are steaming westward. . . ."

---

* Morison, *History of United States Naval Operations in World War II*, Vol. 4.

Yamamoto, realizing Nagumo was completely demoralized, relieved him of command and turned it over to Kondo, who continued to come posthaste up from the southwest. Just before midnight Kondo got off a brave message ordering all ships to prepare for a night battle.

But in the early hours of June 5 Yamamoto thought better of what was shaping up. He had hoped the Americans would come on west within range of his powerful guns, but they appeared to be resisting the invitation to destruction. Apart from Nagumo's silly reports, there was no solid intelligence on the composition and location of the American force.

As it finally broke over Yamamoto that his four magnificent carriers were gone, he apparently went into a state of deep depression. If his surface forces kept probing after the Americans, it was more likely they would become the victims of a dawn air attack than the victors of a night battle. At 0255 he ordered abandonment of the Midway invasion and a general retirement to the west.

Meantime Spruance slept soundly.

He had resisted urging to go on west and close the enemy. Though he did not know *Yamato* was out there, he knew there were battleships whose big guns fired as accurately at night as by daylight. The risk was not worth it. Instead, he wanted to be in a position next morning where he could oppose a Midway invasion or resume contact with enemy naval forces. He decided to keep moving to avoid submarines, heading east until midnight, turning north for an hour and then going west.

At 0045 in the dark morning of June 5 the staff watch officer on *Enterprise* received a report of a surface radar contact 14 miles to the northwest. It might be the feared enemy force. He ordered an emergency turn to the east, sent a destroyer to investigate and called the admiral in his cabin. Under similar circumstances Halsey probably would have ordered General Quarters.

But Spruance yawned. "Very well," he told the watch officer. "When you lose the contact, resume the base course and speed. Good night."

At 0400 Spruance was awakened again. The submarine *Tambor*, 90 miles west of Midway, had made contact with a group of ships. Her skipper, Lieutenant Commander John Murphy, reported "many unidentified ships" to Admiral English at Pearl Harbor, but did not give a course. Spruance's son Edward was aboard *Tambor* as a junior officer. The vagueness of the message irritated the admiral, as it did everyone at Pearl. Lacking more specific information, everyone assumed the Japanese invasion force was heading for Midway. Submarines were brought in close to the atoll, and Spruance kept his fleet hovering north of Midway awaiting developments.

Murphy finally got off another report about 0600 identifying the ships as *Mogami*-class cruisers on a westerly course. Actually there were four cruisers and two detroyers participating in the general withdrawal Yamamoto had ordered. *Tambor* never did get off a torpedo at them. But a Japanese lookout spotted her periscope and in the ensuing evasive action *Mogami* was badly damaged when she and *Mikuma* rammed together.

Tambor's bumbling was typical of the poor performance displayed by submarines at the Battle of Midway—and unlike the excellent work the submarine service would perform later in the war. The skippers blamed English for a poor disposition of the force, and he blamed them for lacking aggressiveness.

Fog and showers enveloped the American fleet in the gray morning light of June 5. Reports from search planes were spotty, but by midmorning Spruance concluded the Japanese were withdrawing in two groups—one to the west and the other to the northwest. He decided to go after the latter. By early afternoon, however, the searchers had lost contact with the enemy, and his whereabouts was sheer guesswork.

Nevertheless, Browning wanted to get off a 1400 launch with heavy bombs, based on the last reported Japanese position. Spruance naturally had to assume that Browning was a competent air officer, though disorganized when it came to detail, and so agreed to the strike. The strike order had no sooner been issued, however, than McClusky, a squadron commander and the *Enterprise* skipper, Captain George D. Murray, stormed onto the bridge, shouting that the order was plain suicide for the pilots. Browning lost his notorious temper and began shouting back that an order was an order.

Their voices rose ever louder until they seemed on the verge of throwing punches. Then Spruance pressed into their midst and told them to cool it.

The young squadron commander looked at him, eyes filling with angry tears: "Admiral, we'll go if *you* tell us to. But if we go, we won't be coming back."

Spruance turned to McClusky without glancing at Browning: "I'll do what you want. The order is cancelled."

As the three officers hurried away, Browning let out a whinny of rage and cried out that he had been insulted. His face looked ashen. Slamming out of the flag shelter, he raced to the bridge deck below. But his voice rose to the shaken staff officers as his cursing became an incoherent screaming and finally he burst into tears. Then there was silence, and everyone in the flag shelter pretended to be very busy. At last someone went below and prevailed on Browning to leave his cabin and return to duty.*

Everyone tried to act as if nothing had happened, and Spruance went out of his way to be courteous to Browning. He had lost faith in him, but he never made any complaint against him and, indeed, praised him both officially and privately. He felt that his attitude,

---

* Buell, *The Quiet Warrior.*

typical of many career officers, was for the good of the service. Thus he did not mention the incident even in interviews with his biographer Buell.*

Though searchers still had not located the enemy, a launch was made at 1500 with lighter bombs. The bombers found only one destroyer, which they attacked unsuccessfully. Darkness fell before many of the planes had returned. Spruance, ignoring fears of submarine attack, ordered *Enterprise* lighted up like a Christmas tree to bring the pilots safely home in darkness. The pilots never forgot it and swore by him for the rest of their time in service.

Dawn of June 6 brought good news. Search planes reported two separate groups of battleships, cruisers and destroyers about 130 miles to the southwest and steaming slowly toward Japan. Spruance ordered the searchers to maintain contact with the enemy while his carriers prepared attacks. What the American planes actually found were the cruisers *Mogami* and *Mikuma,* which had been damaged in collision after being frightened by *Tambor*'s periscope.

It took three American attacks to put *Mikuma* under in the afternoon and send *Mogami* creeping away badly crippled.

Detailed information about the battle still was incomplete. Spruance believed he had sunk three enemy carriers, but did not yet know the fourth had gone down too. Nimitz at Pearl believed the same.

Then came an eye-witness account from the unsinkable Ensign Gay, who had not expected to live and tell his account of historic events. While paddling about in his lifejacket and trying to be optimistic about his fate he had watched three enemy carriers sink and seen the fourth so badly damaged that she was bound to go under.

---

* Other historians, such as Morison, do not mention Browning's lapse in efficiency or emotional outburst, perhaps because there is no official record of such events.

And then, miraculously, he had been spotted by a Catalina flying boat and was rescued; the report of what he had seen was sent to Pearl.

Gay's story confirmed Nimitz's belief that the Japanese had lost all four of their carriers. He urged Spruance to press on and destroy as many surface vessels as possible. Which was precisely what Spruance was trying to do.

After *Yorktown* was hit badly in June 4 battle and had lost her power, Captain Elliott Buckmaster ordered Abandon Ship in the belief the carrier was about to capsize. It is believed not a single member of the crew of 2,270 was lost in the transfer to destroyers which gathered round. The abandonment was orderly—even merry. Men floating in life jackets yelled "Taxi! Taxi!" to rescuing destroyers, while a group on one life-raft sang "The Beer Barrel Polka."

When darkness fell no one expected to see a trace of *Yorktown* at next dawning. But on the morning of June 5 there floated Waltzing Matilda, as unsinkable as Ensign Gay in his life jacket. The efforts of a minesweeper to tow her in a rising sea did not make much headway. At last a large salvage party was put aboard her before dawn of June 6. These men, toiling without pause, put out the one remaining fire and corrected her list with the aid of power pumps on the destroyer *Hammann,* which was lashed alongside the carrier. By early afternoon the salvage party was positive that *Yorktown* could be saved and floated back to Pearl.

The day previously a Japanese search plane had seen her afloat. When Yamamoto received the report he ordered submarine *I-168* to go get *Yorktown.* The task was made difficult because the searcher gave an erroneous position, but *I-168* persisted in her stealthy hunt. Early in the afternoon of June 6 the submarine finally sighted the carrier with destroyer *Hammann* alongside. There seemed little chance that *I-168* could sneak in for a kill through a screen of five American destroyers maintaining a constant patrol on a radius of 2,000 yards from *Yorktown.*

The crews of these destroyers were no amateurs; they were veterans of anti-submarine warfare in the Atlantic and equipped with echo-ranging sound gear. Sound conditions were poor, however, because of oil slicks and flotsam from the carrier. Stealthily, skillfully *I-168* crept through the destroyer screen and quickly fired off four torpedoes. One missed, two passed beneath *Hammann* and exploded on *Yorktown.* The fourth split *Hammann* in two; she sank in four minutes with large loss of life.

While two destroyers rescued men, three dashed about hunting the attacker and dropping depth charges. *I-168* dived deep and lay silent. That night she got underway and made it safely back to Japan, having chalked up the biggest submarine kill of the Pacific war.

The stubborn salvage party still believed they could save *Yorktown.* They planned to board her again and resume work on the morning of June 7. But the two torpedoes in her entrails proved too much for her. During the night she began to list again, and by dawn's early light it was apparent she was going down forever.

The destroyers stood by like solemn sentinels, colors at half-mast, all hands uncovered and at attention. Waltzing Matilda had seemed as much a great lady as a great ship to many of her crewmen. And her death throes at 0600 seemed almost human. She uttered a sighing sound and rolled over, her tumbling loose gear making a death rattle. Then she sank in two thousand fathoms.

13

Victory

Battles, like old soldiers, never die—they just fade away.

Yamamoto was still trying to fight the battle after Spruance had won it. Nimitz hoped it could be enlarged to yield an even greater victory than the Americans already had gained. So did Spruance, but he was above all prudent and realistic. By being so, he prevented Yamamoto from turning Midway into a draw or possibly a Japanese victory.

When Yamamoto learned on June 6 that Spruance's planes were attacking *Mogami* and *Mikuma,* he formed a new force of six heavy cruisers and a destroyer squadron and ordered them to rendezvous with the stricken cruisers, then attack the American fleet. Yamamoto also called up air reinforcements from the Marshall Islands and told his other forces to close on Spruance if he took the bait of attacking the newly formed cruiser group.

But Spruance saw the hook in the bait and would not lunge for it. He realized the Japanese were trying to draw him within range of their bombers on Wake Island, which would outnumber the American carrier planes. Thus Spruance decided to end the battle. He had fulfilled Nimitz's orders more completely than CINCPAC probably had at first thought possible: the enemy invasion of Midway had been thwarted and four of Japan's finest carriers sunk with the loss of only one American carrier. Now Spruance's destroyers were running low on fuel, his aircraft depleted, his remaining pilots exhausted after three days of fighting. So, instead of going on west, he withdrew his ships to the northeast to refuel.

At last, on June 8, Yamamoto started home despondently. He kept to his cabin and scarcely spoke to anyone. An officer's diary recovered by American intelligence contained this entry: "We are retreating. . . . It is utterly discouraging. . . . The marines, who were showing off, have not even courage to drink beer."

Never before in modern times had a Japanese naval force been defeated.

On the evening of June 6, after three days of alerts and fighting, everyone aboard *Enterprise* shaved, showered and put on fresh uniform. The pilots broke out a private stock of liquor, and Spruance acted as if he didn't know a violation of naval rules was occurring while the pilots had a few shipboard drinks to celebrate their victory. Dinner was festive. Afterwards Spruance and several staff officers sat around the ward room reading the radioed news reports which they had not had time to scan in the past few days.

One news item concerning a bizarre murder in the States prompted a staff officer to remark that murder was such an unnatural act only one with a deranged mind could commit it.

Spruance glanced up from his news sheets and asked dryly, "Just what do you think I've been doing all afternoon?"

Considering the preponderance of Japanese strength at Midway, the American victory was a miracle. American losses were one carrier and one destroyer sunk, 307 men killed, 147 aircraft lost and extensive damage to Midway installations. Japanese losses, on the other hand, were so severe as to change the course of the war in the Pacific: four carriers and one heavy cruiser sunk, another heavy cruiser damaged badly, 322 planes destroyed and 2,500 men killed, including many experienced pilots. Never again did the Japanese mount a serious attack to the east against the Americans.

It was the loss of planes and skilled pilots, as well as carriers, that hit the Japanese hardest. The United States could compensate for its losses in men and materiel as Japan could not because of the greater American reserves in manpower and industry. Midway tipped the scale of the Pacific war in favor of the United States. While there were years of bitter fighting ahead, Japan never recovered its initial advantage.

Admiral Nimitz, collaborating with Professor Potter in writing *Triumph in the Pacific: The Navy's Struggle against Japan* (Englewood Cliffs, N. J.: Prentice-Hall, 1963), said this about the victory:

> Midway was essentially a victory of intelligence. . . . Since the United States was intercepting and reading Japanese coded messages, American intelligence of the enemy's plans was remarkably complete. Nimitz's information indicated the Japanese objectives, the approximate composition of the enemy forces, the direction of approach, and the approximate date of attack. It was this knowledge that made the American victory possible.

Nimitz recommended Rochefort for the Distinguished Service Medal for his role in the Midway victory, but King vetoed it on the grounds too many people had been involved in codebreaking to single out only one. Later Rochefort fell victim to naval bureaucrats with whom he dared to argue. King, in one of his most incredible decisions, ordered Rochefort out of cryptographic service after he refused duty in Washington. Rochefort requested active sea duty. Instead, the Navy's most brilliant cryptographer was put in command of a floating drydock.

Following Midway there were second-guessers, as after every battle, who said Spruance didn't pursue the enemy far or hard enough. But this notion was not shared by Nimitz or officers who knew the risks that had to be run and the odds to overcome. Some officers felt relief that the reflective Spruance rather than the impetuous Halsey had been in command. Yamamoto might have drawn Halsey to disaster as he could not Spruance. Later in the war, in the series of naval battles involving the American invasion of the Philippines, the Japanese easily siphoned off Halsey on a wild good chase. Something similar might have happened at Midway with even more disastrous results.

In his summary of the battle, Morison writes, "Fletcher did well, but Spruance's performance was superb. Calm, collected, decisive, yet receptive to advice; keeping in his mind the picture of widely disparate forces, yet boldly seizing every opening. Raymond A. Spruance emerged from the battle one of the greatest admirals in American naval history."

Spruance was incapable of displaying the ebullience and swagger that make a military leader seem a hero in the eyes of many Americans. He was, as Buell aptly calls him, "the quiet warrior." And a great one, as demonstrated by his role in later events of the Pacific war.

The true heroes of Midway were irked by claims made by the U. S. Army Air Force. Some clever public relations people, embroidering mistaken sightings by bomber crews, made it sound that Air Force planes sank the enemy carriers. Throughout the war many misinformed people believed that Army bombers won the Battle of Midway. That was not so. Army bombers did only slight damage to one enemy vessel and never sank anything throughout the course of the battle.

It was a fact of World War II—not something made up by propagandists—that a boost in public morale was always reflected in greater industrial productivity and more enthusiastic military efforts. Perhaps that was one of the chief accomplishments of the miraculous victory at Midway. It gave a great boost to a people depressed by a long string of defeats.

Acknowledgments

I do not attempt a complete bibliography of the reading and research involved in preparing this book. I cite, rather, main sources which might interest anyone who wants to read further about World War II in the Pacific. The books mentioned should be available in every good public library. If they are not, ask the library to obtain them.

No one who wants to know what the Navy did in World War II can avoid the lively, delightful work of Samuel Eliot Morison. His 15-volume *History of United States Naval Operations in World War II,* published by Little, Brown and Company, tells the story of the Navy's role in both Pacific and European waters from the beginning Battle of the Atlantic in 1939 through Japan's surrender. Morison, an honored historian who died a Rear Admiral in the Naval Reserve, always writes vividly and was present for many of the operations he discusses. He had able assistants and full Navy cooperation in compiling what amounts to an official naval history of the war. For this book I have especially employed Morison's material in Volumes 3 and 4 of the 15-volume history.

If you want to read a less detailed but dramatic account of the naval war, try Morison's *The Two-Ocean War: A Short History of the United States Navy in the Second World War* (Boston: Little, Brown, 1963). I have used information from this book, too.

There is advantage for a biographer and historian to have years of distance from his subject. This is exemplified by the works of E. B. Potter, a professor of history at the U. S. Naval Academy. Potter, a noted historian who served as a naval officer in the Pacific during World War II, became a good friend of Nimitz and collaborated with him on *Sea Power: A Naval History* (Englewood Cliffs, N. J.: Prentice-Hall, 1960), which offers absorbing insights into the Pacific war. I have especially used information Professor Potter offers in his excellent biography *Nimitz* (Annapolis: Naval Institute Press, 1976), which is the authoritative life story of the World War II CINCPAC.

I am equally indebted to Commander Thomas B. Buell, a naval career officer who has created a superb work in *The Quiet Warrior: A Biography of Admiral Raymond A. Spruance* (Boston: Little, Brown, 1974). Almost all the personal quotations and incidents involving Spruance in my book are from *The Quiet Warrior,* as are most of the personal incidents involving the Commander in Chief Pacific Fleet taken from Potter's *Nimitz.*

Another book you should read if interested in the war in the Pacific is *Silent Victory: The U. S. Submarine War against Japan* by Clay Blair, Jr. (Philadelphia and New York: J. B. Lippincott, 1975). It is a fascinating work, meticulously researched.

Time ripens one's judgment of events as much as of people and literature. Time can offer an advantage to the historian who has researched his material diligently over the historian who was at the scene of events in person. This advantage of distance from the scene becomes clear in the works of Potter, Buell and Blair. For example, Morison knew how effectively the U.S. Navy was reading Japanese codes, but he was forbidden to mention it under the security rules at the time of his writing. It troubled his honest historian's desire to tell the whole truth, but secrecy was put to him as a matter of patriotism. And Samuel Eliot Morison was nothing if not a great patriot. After the war had ended, the restrictions really had nothing to do with national security.

These restrictions do not appear in the works of Potter, Buell and Blair. They report facts as they happened. For instance, both Potter and Blair discuss the fascinating subject of codebreaking fully and clearly. I am indebted to them for their information.

I thank these writers for permission to borrow from their work and hail the spirit of Admiral Morison, who not only supplied wonderful facts but knew that history should be *fun* for both writer and reader.

There are several able and interesting general outline histories of World War II. Personally I have enjoyed especially *The Second World War: An Illustrated History* by A. J. P. Taylor (New York: G. P. Putman's Sons, 1975) with its fine maps and photographs.

Above all, the important thing in reading an historical account like this is to go find some better books and enjoy them.

—CHARLES MERCER

New York

Index

The Author

Charles Mercer is the author of more than a score of books besides many stories and articles in national publications. During World War II he served as an intelligence officer in the Pacific and was recalled to active duty in the Korean War. He and his wife live in New York, where he is an editor with a book publishing house.